tonight at 7.30

tonight at 7.30

one family's life at the table

Kristen Frederickson

Avery Curran

First published in UK and USA in 2014 by
Kristen Frederickson

Copyright @ Kristen Frederickson 2014
Images copyright @ Avery Curran 2014

ISBN 978-0-9930868-0-9

Tiitle quotation from *Tonight at 7:30*, a poem by W. H. Auden
in honor of M.F.K. Fisher.

Photography by Avery Curran,
except pp. 14, 15, 17, 81 by Vincent Keith
Designed by Briony Hartley, Goldust Design
Illustrations by Daisy Chandley
Printed and bound in China
by 1010 Printing International Ltd

dedication

We dedicate this book to our beloved friend, the late Jeanne Grieger

contents

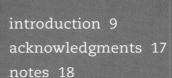

introduction

Two years ago our teenage daughter Avery Curran picked up a camera as I was putting the finishing touches on our family dinner, and in an instant produced an image that elevated the food beyond any photograph I could have achieved. A tremendous amount of practice and a course of photography in Brooklyn later, she is extremely accomplished, with an eye for an unusual point of view and focus that I cannot emulate. For a mother and a teenage daughter, with all the stresses of modern life in place, it is not always easy to find points of common interest. This cookbook has brought us together in the months and years when we needed it the most, and I know its recipes and photographs will bring back warm memories for both of us when Avery is out in the world on her own, with a kitchen and an appetite.

Avery's photography and my cooking have become a true collaboration. When we began our project, I had been taking what I thought were adequate food photographs for my blog, *Kristen in London*, but I was lazy about presentation, feeling that taste should matter more than appearance. Avery rightly pointed out very early in our work together that she could not make a beautiful photograph out of a dish I had not tried to make beautiful. Slowly, my rather slapdash approach to presentation evolved into something more sophisticated, to give her a proper subject to photograph. Her work in turn evolved from an interest only in the artistic nature of the image to a more representative expression of a finished dish, since readers of my blog really wanted to know how they could expect the food to look, if they followed my recipes. Over the years, and after many emails up and down the house asking, "Are you ready to take a picture?" we have learned from each other, my food becoming more of a pleasure to look at, and Avery's photographs making the dishes look quite beautiful, and always tempting.

Our cooking and photography life spans two worlds, dictated by season. Nine years ago, our peaceful life in New York was uprooted when my husband was transferred with his job to London. While this was in some ways a very nice thing to have happen and we were glad to move to our second-favorite city in the world, it did mean a complete change in my daily life. My work as an art historian and gallery owner became part of the past, and because the London art world is a completely different animal from the New York art world, I realized I needed to find another way to work and express myself. The excitement of the London food world, with its foreign ingredients

and outbuildings. I cook very differently in these two places, a bit schizophrenically perhaps, but the contrast works for us and gives us something to look forward to no matter where we are.

In London, I cook comfort food, partly because we're all in need of comfort as we battle through our various challenges: school exams, property development, volunteer work. Life is hectic and the weather often a bit unconsoling, and so long-cooked, creamy, warm food is the order of the day. We often feed other hungry people in need of comfort and sustenance and I have developed flexible recipes that appeal to lots of different sorts of eaters: simple food with a bit of a twist, to keep both children and adults interested.

At Red Gate Farm, I cook much quicker, more seasonal fare, tending toward big salads, seafood, grilled delights and of course corn – on the cob most popularly, but also turning up in bean salads, chowders and casseroles. Meals are taken messily at the old picnic table on the terrace, sunny at lunch and shady at dinner.

Because of the double nature of my cooking life, the photographs take on a different character. Days in London are very short in autumn and winter, and dinner takes place long after the sun has set, so in many cases Avery photographs

and exotic terminology, reached out and grabbed me, and I began writing about food instead of art.

When we moved to London, we decided to keep the little farmhouse in Connecticut that had been our weekend retreat from New York City. While we embraced completely our new life across the pond, we hoped that by retaining Red Gate Farm, we might be able to retain a little of ourselves that is American. The experiment has been successful.

In the hectic, damp, grey months of the school year, then, we live in London. In the hot sultry summers, we decamp to Red Gate Farm: a dilapidated, sun- and humidity-drenched house

London food in a light box, which produces a clear, simple and clean image. Dinners at Red Gate Farm occur in the long hazy evenings of summer, and these photographs are taken in natural light on our crowded picnic table with the red barns and white picket fences in the background.

I love occasions for which I'm allowed to pull out all the stops and cook with abandon, and I can find any reason to celebrate. Our yearly calendar will include a celebration supper after the first brilliant night of the school musical, my own birthday dinner with a table full of girlfriends, a luncheon party for my fellow church bell-ringers,

an expatriate Thanksgiving in London with 20 people around the table and the board groaning, or a snowy New Year's Eve with neighbors in Connecticut. Each school term brings a luncheon to thank the lovely ladies in London who run Avery's school's Lost Property room, and 30 or 40 of us gather in my kitchen to eat and gossip. Many of my favorite party dishes have come out of experiments to feed the volunteers of Lost Property.

Truth be told, though, my favorite occasion is dinner at home with my family, promptly at 7.30 every night we can manage it. There may be extra people to feed: overnight guests tired out from a day of tourism in London, hungry school friends, neighbors willing to try an experimental dish or two. Everyone in both London and Connecticut knows that 7.30 will find us at the table with more than enough food for a guest or two.

The three activities I love the most are playing around with ingredients (I absolutely love food shopping in both countries, and never find it boring or repetitive), eating great food, and talking and writing about food. For me, any experience is left incomplete until I've been able to frame it in words, and it is almost impossible to separate in my mind the joy of cooking something luscious, sitting down with the people I love to enjoy eating it, and finding ways to frame the experience on the page. I strongly believe in dinner conversation because there is nothing nicer than combining a wonderful meal with reminiscences, embellished family stories, political arguments, or just the reassuring telling of the day's events.

Our book is organized by types of dishes: soups, main courses, side dishes, salads, party foods, sauces, desserts. I don't really appreciate the notion of appetizers, because they argue for a more formal way of serving food than mine, with separate courses placed in front of guests, one after the other. I much prefer serving "à la francaise," with dishes from which family and friends can help themselves, taking what they like and in the sort of portion that feels right. The exception to this tendency is soup, with which I sometimes begin a meal (I have fabulous little shot glasses for that course). For this reason, soups appear first in the book.

I believe the best way to cook, if you have the flexibility, is to go with what sounds good on any particular day. If fish seems appealing, dinner can be fried haddock with triple-cooked French fries (a family obsession), or roasted salmon with a spicy, sweet teriyaki sauce, or scallops poached in olive oil and two parsleys. If we are in the mood for a pasta night (this would be every night if it were up to our daughter), then, hearty Bolognese, or creamy carbonara are perfect candidates, or if we're feeling like we need a light meal, farfalle with roasted red peppers, or with broccoli and pine nuts. On a perfectly beastly, rainy London day, surely soup is the answer: smooth Portobello mushroom with Madeira, elegant celeriac with champagne, or if someone has a delicate stomach, Tom Yum chicken soup with medicinal herbs.

When the weather at Red Gate Farm is gloriously sunny and we can't bear to go indoors, of course the grill is indicated, and then we must

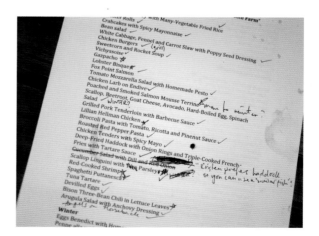

choose between chicken burgers with herbed cheese tucked inside, or little round zucchinis or mushroom caps stuffed with everything under the sun. Sometimes in the summer nothing will do but luxurious shellfish. Nothing beats a steamed lobster dipped in garlicky mayo, its leftover claw turned into a perfect lobster roll for lunch the next day. And to my mind there is nothing more wonderful than a crabcake, studded with red pepper and spring onion.

What about dinner parties? I never fuss and I never fret. I love having people over who come prepared to have a good time, and I like to serve them food that everyone likes: not too challenging for the children present, but food with a twist. Great ideas for dinner parties are a many-vegetable stir-fry with the ever-popular home-fried rice, laden with more vegetables and scrambled egg. Or my all-time favorite dish, chicken meatballs in a golden-pink paprika and sour cream sauce. Four-cheese lasagna is always welcome. Although it's easy to find a ready-made dish of lasagna at the supermarket, this will cater to the lowest common denominator of flavor, and it is all the more delicious to rediscover a homemade, perfect version of a classic dish, made with the best ingredients, and with love.

Because I love to write nearly as much as I love to cook, my bookshelves and bedside tables are filled with the work of food writers who have inspired me. First is the late and much-missed Laurie Colwin, novelist and columnist for Gourmet magazine in my formative decades of the 1970s and 1980s. Her particular brand of opinionated, warm-hearted, highly individualistic descriptions in *Home Cooking: A Writer in the Kitchen* made it all right, even desirable for me to develop my own quirks and obsessions in the kitchen. A generation or two before her, MFK Fisher chronicled her adventures in the kitchen, often under the most challenging of circumstances (*How To Cook a Wolf*

chief among them). Ruth Reichl, in *Tender at the Bone*, describes a bizarre and delicious childhood in ways that I can only admire. I would like to be able to say that my favorite work by the great Lillian Hellman was one of her ground-breaking plays, but the truth is that I will always reach for *Eating Together: Recipes and Recollections* in which she gives us various beloved recipes and tales of the friends with which she shared them.

In fact, all too often I find myself riveted in novels and memoirs not by the fascinating plots or life events, but by what the characters cooked and ate. My enjoyment of the Lord Peter Wimsey mysteries by Dorothy L. Sayers was enhanced greatly by the charming book of recipes, *The Lord Peter Wimsey Cookbook*, written with great love and imagination by William J. Eakin and Elizabeth Bond Ryan. In more recent mystery series, I simply cannot separate my love of the story from my love of the food therein. In this category fall the inimitable Virginia Rich and Katherine Hall Page. How I would have loved to sit down at a table, or shop at the farmer's market, with Mrs. Potter and Faith Fairchild. The combination of storytelling and mouthwatering meals is not to be missed.

I stop every day to appreciate, in the difficult world we see all around us, how fortunate I am

to live in peace, to have enough to eat, and to spend my days messing about in the kitchen and at my desk, feeding the people around me and writing about it so that we remember. Every one of these recipes is laden with associations for me and for my family, and whenever my friends have taken up one of my recipes and made it at home, they report two lovely things: they always work, and they always please. It is an immensely satisfying feeling to feed people proper, generous, delicious food, and I want you to share that feeling, and my recipes.

acknowledgments

I was first inspired to cook by my mother, Suzanne Wedeking Frederickson, in quite a different way than is typical. She did not love to cook and was very happy when I wandered into the kitchen, about age 11. Since then she has been an unfailingly warm support and I am extremely grateful. I thank my mother-in-law Rosemary Curran for giving me honeymoon recipes that are still our favorites today and for being great company in the kitchen.

I am grateful beyond measure to the late Jeanne Grieger and to her daughter Cynthia, for showing me how to be a hostess.

I thank my sister Jill Frederickson and my brother-in-law Joel Grove for their generosity, Kathleen Kucka and John Sutter for their long friendship in several kitchens, our Red Gate Farm neighbors Mike and Lauren Lyons and Judy and Rollie Hannan, our Catskill friends Tony and Olimpia Romero, and our London neighbors Vincent Keith and Peter Carter, Elizabeth Price, Sue Kumleben, John and Suzanne Molloy, Elizabeth Richards, Sara and Selva Ramasamy and Stephanie Conder, who have made us welcome at their tables. I am grateful to my New York sister Alyssa Sadoff who never laughs at my wish to be Jewish, and whose matzoh ball soup is just about the only food I love that I cannot replicate.

My dear father Paul Frederickson and father-in-law Jack Curran were beloved guests at my table, and I miss them more than I can say.

I thank our friends on both sides of the ocean: readers of my blog and Facebook posts who encouraged me in this project. Our "Stillmeadow" neighbors Anne Taber Colby and David and Kate Goewey have been staunch supporters and willing eaters. Their introduction to the work of Gladys Taber gave me faith in the kind of cooking and writing I believe in.

Staci Strauss and Craig McCord with *HandPicked Nation* have, with their support, made me a better cook and writer. The encouragement of *Vintage* Magazine editor Ivy Baer Sherman has been a joy, as has been the help of Heather Holden Brown. My friends at the 2008 Arvon Foundation food-writing course inspire me, most of all Orlando Murrin, Rosie Jones and Sam Goldsmith, who have made this book much better (but they are in no way responsible for my mistakes).

Finally, I thank my husband John Curran who likes to eat everything, and also can fix any technical glitch that comes along. Our daughter Avery Curran's contribution to this book cannot be put into words, so I shall merely thank her for her hours with me in the kitchen and for her beautiful photographs.

general notes to the reader

1. Plain olive oil is perfectly acceptable over more expensive extra virgin, unless specified otherwise. It is really silly to buy expensive oil only to mix it with highly flavored things, or to heat it.

2. Butter should be unsalted.

3. Eggs should be large.

4. Sugar should be granulated/caster, unless specified otherwise.

5. Chocolate should be 60% cocoa content or more.

6. I do not trust ready-ground meat, or ready-"minced" as it is called in Britain. Therefore I grind all my own, using a simple, inexpensive plastic grinder that is easy to clean. It takes about ten minutes to trim meat or chicken and put it through the grinder. While I know that most people buy their meat ready-ground, I would strongly encourage you to grind your own. The texture is much more agreeable and there are none of what my daughter calls "bad bites," which arise from gristle, and your meat is exposed to fewer surfaces outside your own clean home.

7. Always make your own breadcrumbs, just by putting leftover bread in the food processor and pulsing till fine. Regular bread makes heavier breadcrumbs than Panko (Japanese) which I specify in my two meatball recipes (chicken and lamb). Panko is dry and fine and necessary for meatballs, but regular bread crumbs are fine for all other recipes.

8. I am devoted to two seasonings without which I really would struggle to cook: Penzey's Fox Point Seasoning from Wisconsin – a mixture of shallots, chives and scallions that livens any chicken dish – and Maldon salt, a standard English ingredient which is completely affordable there, and ludicrously expensive everywhere else. I mention Fox Point when I use it, and all mentions of "sea salt" assume Maldon; perhaps you have a seasoning blend and salt that have earned your loyalty too.

9. Except in desserts, my measurements are never precise, but are useful guidelines.

some notes about cooking in britain and america

Measurements

The first thing you will notice about recipes written in the UK is that they adhere to the metric system of measurements. That is, the British (and in fact everyone but Americans) use grams instead of ounces, liters instead of quarts, kilograms instead of pounds. But lurking under this seemingly simple translation is a far more complex and maddening issue of volume. Americans like to put things in cups and then take them out again.

But what IS a cup of grated cheese? How tightly packed it is, and what about the fact that Parmesan cheese is much lighter than, say, Cheddar? And don't get me started on the fact that Americans measure dry things in one kind of cup and wet things in another. Growing up there, it all seemed to make perfect sense, but once I've gone out into the world I realize how quixotic American measuring methods are.

Somehow generations of great American cooks have thrived with instructions like "a cup of brown sugar, packed," or "two cups spinach, loosely packed." Americans measure butter by the stick, because that is how it comes, quaintly, in the supermarket. But they all know that a stick of butter is ½ cup and weighs 4 ounces. Therefore, I have been sensible in this book and indicated measurements in ounces where it is easy for American cooks to do this calculation, and have retained "cups" when it makes sense to do so.

I feel a bit amphibious in this, because I respect the accuracy of weighing ingredients on my British scale, but something American in me makes me reach for a nice Pyrex cup when it's time to measure. The truth is that for most of my recipes, measurements are only broad guidelines. The exception to this is desserts, which make me so nervous that I always measure exactly, and perhaps you should too.

Naming things

Winston Churchill's famously observed that America and Britain are "two peoples separated by a common language." Nowhere is this more evident than in the world of food. I once sent my husband to the greengrocer in London to buy endive. I pronounced this in the American way, "en-dive," properly butchering the original French. He called up. "They don't have any. They don't even know what en-dive is." "Try 'ahn-deev,'" I advised. "No luck," he reported. "How about 'chicory'?" I suggested. A brief pause. "Got it."

Here I give you some translations that will be helpful in my recipes.

Naming vegetables

I love cilantro, which word Americans use because of our proximity to Mexico. To get cilantro in Britain you must ask for coriander, which harkens back to old French. In British cooking, coriander seed (often ready-ground) are a more popular seasoning than in America, because of coriander's place in Indian cooking.

Many food terms in Britain arise from French. Courgettes are what the British call zucchini, and aubergines are eggplants. Arugula in America is supposed to be the same as rocket in Britain, and it looks similar and can be used interchangeably in my recipes. However, Americans don't like the same level of bitterness in their lettuce leaves and so arugula has been bred to be much more benign than rocket, which is quite peppery. I miss rocket when I am in America.

Americans cook with scallions and the British with spring onions, and they are the same. Shallots are the same, too, but the British pronounce them like "The Lady Of," where Americans place the emphasis on the first syllable.

Fruits and vegetables in Britain often come in small boxes called punnets, and while there is no standard measurement for the quantity in them, we all feel we know what amount is meant by a punnet of mushrooms.

Naming meat

What Americans call tenderloin steaks are in Britain called fillet steaks, and because of the complex relationship between Britian and France, the "t" which is silent in America is pronounced firmly in Britain.

Bacon in Britain is, unless specified otherwise, a completely meaty cut of pork that resembles what in America is called Canadian bacon. To get in Britain what Americans think of as bacon, one must ask for streaky bacon. Bacon comes in slices called rashers.

Baking terms

Recipes in Britain that call for caster sugar can be made without a problem in America with granulated sugar, but caster's texture is closer to the American super-fine sugar. For my recipes, there is no important difference.

Baking soda in America is bicarbonate of soda in Britain. All-purpose flour in America is plain flour in Britain, meaning that leavening must be added in both countries. Cake flour in America is more finely milled than plain flour, but British plain flour is already more finely milled than American plain flour, so no adjustments need necessarily be made in the UK when an American recipe calls for cake flour. If you feel concerned, however, 2 tbsps of cornflour (cornstarch in America) may be added to each cup of plain flour to further simulate cake flour.

Dairy

British cream comes in several levels of fat content, as cream does in America. American half-and-half contains the lowest level of fat in any of the two countries' cream products, about 14%. Slightly richer than this are British single cream and American light cream, which are interchangeable in my recipes. Even richer, as the names imply, are British whipping cream and American whipping cream, which are interchangeable in my recipes. Still fattier is American heavy whipping cream, and fattiest (and therefore most delicious) of all is British double cream. These last two are interchangeable in my recipes.

The British have soured cream and the Americans sour cream and they are interchangeable in my recipes. However, the British version is higher in fat content and therefore I tend to use half-fat soured cream in my sauces to avoid a puddle of fat on the surface (something that doesn't bother me but might my guests).

Because of its proximity to France, British grocery stores nearly always contain crème fraîche, which is similar to American sour cream although less sour. They can be used interchangeable in my recipes, and crème fraîche is beginning to appear in American shops. Thickest of all (as the name suggests) is clotted cream which traditionally comes from Devonshire and is used exclusively in sweet dishes.

I am very lucky to have the chance to cook in both countries, and I appreciate the different charms and strengths of each place. Animals are less intensively reared in Britain and so it is easier to find very high quality, humanely-raised meat and chicken there. Raw (unpasteurized) dairy products are more routinely available in Britain than in America. Most fun of all is the presence on shop shelves of foreign ingredients from the many places where Britain had colonies, and from the nearby European countries. Shopping in Britain is always an adventure.

When I come "home" to America, though, what I crave is the familiarity of summertime treats like big juicy tomatoes, dozens and dozens of ears of corn on the cob (called sweetcorn in Britain), and fresh Maine lobsters, recently so plentiful that they are cheaper than most meats. My daughter longs all year for the giant half-sour pickles to be had in America, and when I arrive I run straight to the deli counter of the supermarket to pick them up and to buy thin-sliced rare roast beef and white American cheese, which comes in long creamy slabs and is sliced for me on the spot. Gone is my interest in the exotic Italian pancettas and triple crème goat cheeses of Europe. Until we go back "home" to Britain.

soups

Our family is devoted to soup. I've yet to meet a vegetable I don't like simmered in stock and pureed with a drizzle of cream. We also love chunky stews in cool weather, and exotic Thai broth when we want to blow our heads off with chili peppers. Soups don't have to be posh, though; it is satisfying to my practical Midwestern side to know that any leftover roasted meat or vegetable can be turned into a delicious meal.

I am not a great believer in appetizers but I do like to offer a taste of an elegant soup in a shot glass, as guests are milling around chatting with friends and sipping something. Soups are casual and welcoming and set a relaxed tone for the meal to come.

Homemade stock is a must in your kitchen. It is very simple, and reassuringly thrifty, to keep back all bones from roasted birds and any slightly tired vegetables in your refrigerator (as well as vegetable trimmings and peelings) and keep a stockpot simmering on your stove.

Any of these soups can be made with vegetable stock for vegetarians, and cream can be left out or substituted with soya milk, for vegans.

basic stock

Some people swear by stock made from a fresh, raw bird. This method involves covering the bird with water, surrounded by whole, fresh vegetables. The bird is cooked just until the meat is edible, then the meat is removed and set aside and the stock left to simmer until flavorful. The result is perhaps a lighter, cleaner stock than what you get from roasted bones, and it's delicious as well. Whether you begin with a roasted carcass or a fresh bird, you will appreciate the goodness of homemade stock.

(serves 4)

bones of any roasted bird – chicken, duck, turkey, guinea fowl

carrots, onions, celery and garlic (along with skins and roots of these)

black peppercorns and sea salt (enough to fill the space of your cupped hand)

splash of Madeira or Marsala wine

Place everything in a large pot and cover with water, then add another two inches of water. Bring to a simmer and leave as long on the stovetop as you can, or place in a very low (150°F/80°C) oven overnight. Strain through a colander and discard solids.

sweetcorn and rocket soup with white crab

Several years ago, I was on a television cooking contest called *Britain's Best Dish*. The parameters for application were simple: to choose which course to cook, and then to submit an entirely original recipe, as far as one knew. I submitted a soup, to the "starter" (British for appetizer) course competition, an invention that combined many of my favorite ingredients, including "rocket," which is known in America as "arugula" but seldom has the intensely sharp bite of its European cousins. This lovely green, cooked in homemade chicken stock with fresh corn cut from the cob (called "sweetcorn" in Britain) and nicely pureed with a bit of cream, then topped with a spoonful of rich white crabmeat, makes for a lovely summer soup. I cooked it so many times in advance of the competition that my family declared it off the menu for quite a long time. But when we got back to it, we all declared it to be a triumph once again. And I won the first round of the telly competition.

(serves 4)

2 tbsps butter

4 cloves garlic, sliced

2 shallots, sliced

4 ears corn, kernels cut off (this yields about 13oz/375g)

3 cups/720ml chicken stock

about 6 cups/120g loosely packed rocket/arugula

½ cup/125ml cream

12oz/340g white crabmeat

Melt butter in heavy stockpot and saute garlic and shallot just until soft, then add corn and cover with stock. Simmer high for about 10 minutes, then add rocket and stir until the rocket has wilted. Blend with hand blender, stir in cream, and pass through a coarse or fine as you like. I find that the best way to get soup through a sieve is to put the stockpot that is your destination pot into the sink, pour the soup into it through the sieve, and then SHAKE the sieve gently till the solids are left behind. It's a bit messier than just stirring (hence the sink), but it's much faster.

Just before serving, place shallow bowls in a warm oven to take the chill off. Quickly ladle soup into each bowl and divide the crabmeat among the bowls. Serve immediately.

vichyssoise

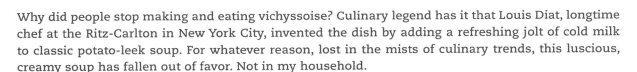

Why did people stop making and eating vichyssoise? Culinary legend has it that Louis Diat, longtime chef at the Ritz-Carlton in New York City, invented the dish by adding a refreshing jolt of cold milk to classic potato-leek soup. For whatever reason, lost in the mists of culinary trends, this luscious, creamy soup has fallen out of favor. Not in my household.

I was introduced to vichyssoise in the New Jersey kitchen of my dear friends Jeanne and Cynthia. Served in deep-green porcelain bowls in the shape of lettuce leaves, it was a revelation of liquid velvet, as close to frozen as a liquid can be, flecked with finely snipped chives, creamy and luxurious.

(serves at least 8)

3 tbsps butter

6 well-cleaned leeks, good white and light green parts, chopped

1 large white onion, cut in eighths

6 medium potatoes (about 1½ lbs/600g), peeled and cut in bite-size chunks

48 fluid oz/1.5 liters commercial chicken broth, or mild homemade stock

dash white pepper

2 cups/500ml cream

chopped chives to garnish

Melt the butter in a heavy stockpot and throw in the leeks, onions and potatoes. Stir until leeks are translucent, then cover in chicken broth and simmer for about 45 minutes until potatoes are tender.

Liquidize with a hand blender and mix in cream and milk, then pass through a sieve into another stockpot into a large bowl. Refrigerate the soup overnight or for at least six hours in the freezer (if it freezes partly, simply stir until chunks melt) and then garnish with chives to serve.

christmas eve oyster stew

This stew is a tradition in my husband's Italian-Irish family. My parents-in-law came to visit us in London the first Christmas after we were married, and I went proudly to the fishmonger to pick up the many oysters I had ordered. Unfortunately I had forgotten to specify "shucked." I carried the enormous tray of oysters in the shell to our flat, and we spent a hilarious and quite dangerous Christmas Eve trying out every tool in the household to try to open those oysters. This is a skill best left to professionals, we concluded. I rejoice in every Christmas that finds my mother-in-law in my kitchen, chopping celery with me, enjoying the memories.

(serves 8 generously)

6 tbsps butter

4 tbsps flour

6 cloves garlic, finely chopped

6 stalks celery, finely finely chopped

1 white onion, finely finely chopped

36–48 shucked oysters with their liquor

4 cups/1 liter whole milk

2 cups/500ml heavy cream

about 1 tbsp celery salt

1 tsp Tabasco

juice of ½ lemon

white pepper to taste

In a large heavy stockpot, melt the butter, then add flour and cook till frothy but not brown. Add garlic, celery and onion and saute until slightly soft, then add oysters with liquor. Stir over medium heat until the edges of the oysters curl up (this means they are nearly cooked).

Add milk and cream, and heat gently until the broth is hot. Take great care to avoid the stew boiling or even simmering as too much heat will curdle the stew. Add the celery salt and taste. Add the Tabasco, lemon juice and pepper, then take off the heat and let the stew sit for 30 minutes or so. Taste again and adjust seasonings. Serve hot with oyster crackers or Saltines.

pink gazpacho

I love this recipe because it came from my friend Jeanne's old-fashioned, white-tiled New Jersey kitchen. I have never been particularly keen on the chunky variety of gazpacho which seems to me to argue for a bowl of tortilla chips on the side. But this version is blended together in a very pleasing way, with enough texture from the nuts and bread to give it interest, and a fresh pink color. The chilling process will go much faster if the chicken stock is chilled first.

(serves at least 8)

1 cup slivered almonds or pine nuts

2 pieces white or wheat bread

6 fresh plum tomatoes, cut in quarters, or 1 x 15oz/400g can peeled plum tomatoes

1 long or 2 small cucumbers

½ cup/125ml cider vinegar

1 tbsp ground cumin

1 tbsp ground cloves

½ tsp chili pepper or cayenne

salt and pepper to taste

2 cups/500ml chicken broth

1 cup/250ml half and half

1 avocado, peeled and stoned, cut in small bite-size pieces

Pulverize the almonds or pine nuts in your food processor, then whiz in the bread. Add the tomatoes, cucumber, oil and vinegar and spices and pulverize until smooth. Depending on the capacity of your processor, you may have to add the tomatoes in batches.

Pour into a very large bowl and add the chicken broth and half and half and blend well. Taste it and add more of whatever the spices or salt you think is needed. Chill thoroughly and serve with avocado pieces mounded in the center.

red pepper soup

This bright red elixir is the ultimate comfort soup. It has an almost smoky flavor, hard to explain since the peppers are not roasted first, but in this recipe you can well imagine how red peppers become paprika. The soup is a wonderful way to deliver a great deal of red pepper goodness without your customers realizing quite how much nutrition is packed into each creamy spoonful. When my little daughter had very unpleasant dental surgery many years ago, this soup was her first request upon returning home, even above ice cream.

(serves at least 4)

2 tbsps butter

3 cloves garlic, roughly chopped

1 shallot, roughly chopped

4 red bell peppers, roughly chopped

several stalks fresh thyme, leaves picked

good splash Madeira or Marsala wine

3 cups/750ml vegetable or chicken stock

½ cup/125ml cream

sea salt and black pepper to taste

Melt the butter in a heavy saucepan and throw in garlic, shallots, peppers and thyme. Saute till softened. Add Marsala and turn up heat to burn off alcohol for 30 seconds or so. Add chicken stock and simmer until peppers are cooked, about 25 minutes. Whizz with a hand blender and put through a sieve to catch pepper skins and thyme stems. Add cream to soup, season and serve hot.

celeriac soup with champagne and fresh thyme

Nearly ten years ago I found myself at the Marylebone Farmer's Market in London, and encountered a large, bulbous, unattractive vegetable about the size of a bowling ball, labelled "celeriac." In America it is more commonly called "celery root." It is what's growing in the ground underneath a head of celery, and since I am inordinately fond of celery I brought it home. I decided that the safest thing to do with it was to cook it in chicken stock and puree it. I expected that it might be slightly stringy, as celery itself is, and could not have been more delighted with the perfectly smooth, velvety result. The earthy flavor is brought out by the addition of a bit of leftover champagne (should such a thing ever appear in your kitchen), but inexpensive white wine will do as well.

(serves 4)

2 tbsps butter

1 celeriac root, peeled and cubed

3 cloves garlic, smashed

1 banana shallot, cut in chunks

several stalks of fresh thyme, leaves picked

good splash champagne

3 cups/750ml chicken stock

½ cup/125ml whipping cream

sea salt and fresh ground pepper to taste

Melt the butter in a heavy saucepan and saute the celeriac, garlic, shallots and thyme till the garlic is slightly soft. Pour in the champagne and simmer for a minute or two. Cover the vegetables with stock and simmer for about 20 minutes or until you can pierce the celeriac easily with a knife. Puree with a hand blender and add cream. Season to taste and serve.

creamy mushroom soup with marsala

We have all had the experience of finding in the fridge part of a box of mushrooms. No dish that I cook seems to call for the whole box – in Britain called a "punnet," a word I love – or it calls for a box and a half, and the rest of the mushrooms languish in the crisper drawer. This soup embraces the leftover mushrooms, as well as any varieties you happen to have on hand: Portobello, chestnut, or the ordinary button kind. It is an old-fashioned soup for a rainy day.

(serves at least 4)

3 tbsps butter

1 white onion, roughly chopped

4 cloves garlic, roughly chopped

1lb/450g mushrooms, any sort you like, roughly chopped

3 cups/750ml chicken stock

good splash Madeira or Marsala wine

several stalks of fresh thyme, leaves picked

½ cup/125ml single cream

sea salt and fresh black pepper to taste

Saute the onions, garlic and mushrooms in the butter until slightly softened, then pour over the stock and Madeira or Marsala and thyme, simmer until mushrooms are soft. Whizz with your hand blender and add the cream. Season to taste and serve hot.

united states senate bean soup

The Senate cafeteria has featured this soup for over 100 years. My mother-in-law Rosemary gave me the recipe, and described her newly-married Sunday-Tuesday cooking ritual. "We went on a serious rotation – Sunday ham, Monday ham sandwiches, Tuesday United States Senate Bean Soup . . . until I couldn't do it one more time." Indeed, you will need to have roasted and eaten a ham, or a ham hock or knuckle, the day before you make the soup, if you want to be authentic. If you are desperate to make this soup without that previous meal, you could substitute ready-cooked ham in chunks and a good canned beef stock, but it won't be quite the same.

(serves 8)

4 cups/32oz/900g Navy beans/haricot/ flageolet

1 ham hock bone with meat still clinging to it

4 medium potatoes, unpeeled

4 stalks celery, chopped

2 white onions

4 cloves garlic, finely chopped

large handful parsley, chopped

Bring the ham hock and beans to a boil in a large stockpot covered with water along with any juices left behind from roasting the ham itself. Meanwhile, boil the potatoes until soft, then drain and mash. Add the potatoes to the ham liquid and mix thoroughly. Bring to the boil again and add the chopped vegetables and the parsley. Bring to the boil one more time and simmer for at least an hour. When nearly ready to serve, take the ham hock out and when cool enough to handle, take the usable meat from it and add in bite-sized pieces to the broth. Serve with crusty bread to soak up juices.

chicken penicillin soup

I have long been an advocate of the view that homemade chicken soup is medicinal. It doesn't really matter to me whether anyone else believes this (although my family do), because simply the cooking aromas and then the flavors of chicken soup make me feel better. I am lucky enough to have a husband to make this soup for me when I occasionally wake up unwell.

I was thrilled when we were in Berlin recently to come across this lovely billboard outside a restaurant. I loved the idea of a cook in modern-day Germany picking up the notion that Jewish cooks have always held: chicken soup as penicillin.

(serves at least 8)

1 large roasting chicken

3 carrots, unpeeled, cut into chunks

1 onion, unpeeled, cut into chunks

3 stalks celery, cut into chunks

3 carrots, peeled and cut into disks

1 onion, peeled and diced

3 stalks celery, chopped roughly

6 cloves garlic, 3 whole, 3 finely chopped

2 large handfuls flat-leaf parsley, leaves only, chopped

1 handful fresh dill, chopped

sea salt and fresh black pepper to taste

Remove the breasts from the chicken and set aside. Place the rest of the chicken into a large stockpot and cover with water. Add the first group of the carrots, onions and celery, and the 3 whole garlic cloves, plus half the parsley and dill. Bring to a simmer and cook for as long as you reasonably can, but at least 3 hours.

While the soup is cooking, slice the chicken breasts very thin and set them aside in the fridge.

When the soup has cooked as long as it can, strain it through a colander into another stockpot. Add the remaining carrots, onions and celery to the broth (keeping the parsley and dill out until the end). Bring to a simmer and season well. When the vegetables are soft (about 20 minutes) add the chicken breast slices and poach gently until just cooked, about 2 minutes. Top with the remaining parsley and dill and serve with comforting crackers, Saltines or Tucs.

Hühnersupp
Penicillin
dun son cin

tom yum paste and soup

(serves 4)

For the paste:

1 stalk lemongrass, lightly crushed, or zest of 1 lemon

1-inch knob of ginger, peeled

2 cloves garlic

2 Kaffir lime leaves sliced thinly, or zest of 1 lime

1 tbsp Thai roasted chili paste or chili garlic sauce

2–4 Thai bird's eye chilies, to taste

2 tbsps Thai fish sauce

juice of 1 lime

1 banana shallot, peeled and cut into chunks

pinch sugar

handful cilantro/coriander with stems

for the soup:

1 x 13oz/400ml can coconut milk

2 cups/500ml fish or chicken stock

1lb/400g raw peeled shrimp, or chicken breast thinly sliced on the bias

8 chestnut mushrooms, thinly sliced

1 bunch scallions/spring onions, thinly sliced both white and green part

1–2 chopped red hot chilies, to taste

handful cilantro/coriander leaves for garnish

Thai chili oil (optional)

One night I had promised my husband Tom Yum Soup for dinner, only to find that I had no jar of Tom Yum Paste in my fridge. It was simple to look up a recipe for the paste, and heartening to discover that I had everything but the lemongrass in my pantry already, and lemon zest worked rather well as a substitute. The soup is now one of the most requested at our house, and you can decide for yourself each time how hot and spicy you want to make it. Shrimp and chicken are both delightful in the soup, but neither is necessary, and it is both vegetarian and vegan without. I am not a tofu person, but if you are, this soup was made for it. If you can find a jar of Thai chili oil, buy it and follow the tradition of drizzling some on your soup. Be judicious.

For the paste: Place everything in your food processor and process till as smooth as you can get it. This paste can be used for curry sauces or soup.

For the soup: Place the paste and all the ingredients for the soup up to the cilantro in a saucepan and bring to a simmer.

Cook very gently until shrimp or chicken are just cooked, perhaps 2 minutes. Top with cilantro and serve hot.

new england clam chowder

For several years before we acquired Red Gate Farm, our summers were spent on Little Cranberry Island, Maine, off the coast of Mount Desert. Little Cranberry is also called Islesford, and the Islesford Dock Restaurant is a real destination. Owned by our old friends Cynthia and Dan Lief, it is a haven of warmth, friendship, magnificent sunsets and exceptional food. My favorite dish there by far is the clam chowder, and while I cannot supply the sunsets, this recipe will make you think you're in Maine. Ready-chopped clams are perfectly good in this soup, but I would recommend the fresh vacuum-packed rather than canned, if you can get them.

(serves at least 6–8)

50 littleneck clams

½ cup/118ml white wine

4 whole stems fresh thyme

4 medium potatoes/1lb/400g, peeled and diced

3 tbsps butter

4 stalks celery, chopped fine

1 white onion, chopped fine

8 stems fresh thyme, leaves picked

3 quarts/2.8 liters whole milk

1 cup/236ml heavy cream

sea salt and fresh black pepper to taste

flat-leaf parsley to garnish, chopped

Place clams in a large bowl and cover with fresh, cold water. Leave for 20 minutes, then drain in a colander. Bring the wine to a boil in a large, heavy-bottomed saucepan or stockpot with a close-fitting lid. Place the clams in the wine and cover. Steam the clams until they open, which they will begin to do in about 10 minutes. Remove the lid and with tongs begin lifting out the clams that have opened, and others will open as you do so. Discard any that do not open. Rinse stockpot and dry thoroughly.

Cool clams until you can handle them. Meanwhile, melt butter in the stockpot and saute celery, onion, thyme leaves and potatoes for 2 minutes. Cover with milk and cream and season to taste. Add clam liquid of you like. Simmer very low until potatoes are soft, about 15 minutes.

While chowder is simmering, take the clams from their shells and remove the hard "mantle" and attached innards and discard them. Rinse the clam that remains (the belly and foot) and chop as coarse or fine as you like. Add the clams to the chowder and stir to mix. Heat very gently before serving. Garnish with a few chopped clams and a bit of chopped parsley.

chicken meatballs with "Pojarski" sauce 52

slow-braised chicken thighs with capers, white wine, bay and olive oil 54

sautéed parcels of chicken stuffed with mozzarella, spinach and bacon 57

chicken burgers with goat cheese and spring onions 58

slow-braised whole chicken with root vegetables 61

chicken tenders with spicy mayo 63

chicken larb on butter/Little Gem lettuce 65

chicken sausages with feta, red onion and chives 66

lillian hellman chicken 69

mama nel's buttermilk herbed chicken 70

simple chicken and broccoli stir-fry with mushroom fried rice 72

chicken livers with mushrooms on toast 75

roasted duck on a pancake with plum sauce 76

roasted guinea fowl with rosemary and 30 cloves of garlic 79

herb-brined roasted turkey 80

poultry

British chicken is less intensely reared than common American brands and it is easier in the UK to buy high-quality chicken without paying unbelievable prices for organic birds. In America, I buy organic chicken in order to achieve the texture and flavor I want, and to ensure that the chickens we eat have had pleasant lives. I like to imagine a day in which there are no chickens available to buy that have been inhumanely raised.

It is important to avoid the very large and ubiquitous American chicken producers in favor of small brands who adhere to high standards for quality of life. Ducks and guinea fowls, being much less popular than chicken in both the US and the UK, are not so tempting to producers to rear intensively and so any brand you might find will have been kindly reared.

chicken meatballs with "Pojarski" sauce

This dish spans three continents and over 100 years. In the 1961 edition of the *New York Times Cookbook*, editor Craig Claiborne included a recipe for "Chicken Cutlets Pojarski," a dish named for a Russian tavernkeeper and cook who produced it for the Tsar. The method involves mixing minced chicken with quantities of melted butter, then breading them and frying them in more butter, and serving them with a paprika sauce. My friend Jeanne introduced me to the dish in New Jersey 20 years ago, and since then in my London kitchen I've adapted it by dropping the butter, changing the cutlets to chicken meatballs, and making the sauce the star.

Rich with sour cream, spiked with brandy and flecked with fresh thyme, this sauce is a show-stopper and the whole dish our family's favorite both for celebration and comfort. Upon going back to look at the original recipe, we were surprised to see that "Pojarski" refers to the cutlets' method, not to the sauce. To us, "Pojarski" means the sauce, and with apologies to Russia, I use it as such here.

(serves 8)

for the meatballs:

2lbs/1kg chicken breasts, boneless and skinless

1½ cup/360ml milk

1½ cup/75g Panko breadcrumbs

1 tbsp Fox Point (or other poultry seasoning)

fresh black pepper

for the sauce:

3 tbsps butter

1 tbsp flour (more later if needed to thicken sauce)

6 cloves garlic, finely chopped

1 shallot, finely chopped

1½ tbsp paprika (I know it sounds a lot)

handful fresh thyme leaves

1/3 cup/90ml brandy

1 cup/240ml chicken stock

1 cup/250ml sour cream

fresh black pepper

Trim the chicken breasts completely of any fat, gristle, or tendons. Place in food processor and pulse until chopped but not mushy. Mix the milk, breadcrumbs and seasonings in a medium bowl, then add the chicken. Combine until well-mixed, adding as much milk as can be absorbed and still have the mixture form loose balls. Set mixture aside.

In a large (at least 12 inches/30cm wide) frying pan or paella pan, melt the butter, add the flour and cook, stirring constantly, for a minute. Then add the garlic and shallots and sauté until soft. Sprinkle on the paprika and fresh thyme and cook for a minute or so. Deglaze the pan with the brandy and cook for two minutes rather high, stirring as the brandy evaporates. Add the chicken stock and sour cream and begin stirring with a rubber whisk. Simmer and season with black pepper to taste.

When the sauce is thoroughly mixed and hot, carefully make meatballs the size of golfballs and drop them gently into the simmering sauce in a single layer. Poach at a low simmer for about five minutes, then turn each meatball carefully, and poach a further five minutes. At this point you may take the pan off the heat and leave it for the flavors to develop. Heat through when you are ready to eat. Serve with noodles or rice.

Stopping At Pojarski's

By CRAIG CLAIBORNE

Once upon a time, according to legend, there was a small and prosperous town between Moscow and St. Petersburg called Torjok. Travelers changed horses there. And in the town was a tavern. The tavernkeeper was named Pojarski and the specialty of the house was an excellent dish made of finely chopped meat, shaped like a cutlet and sauteed. Called *Pojarskiya kotleti* or *Pojarski* cutlet, the owner made his dish of game or of game and beef together. Today it is usually made of chicken. The recipe with chicken is given here, and it is accompanied by recipes for a paprika sauce, sauteed carrots, noodles and salad. An outline for a complete menu is given on Page 112.

slow-braised chicken thighs with capers, olives white wine, bay and olive oil

Once a school term, I invite the Ladies of Lost Property – my volunteers in the never-ending attempt to reunite girls with their property – to a sumptuous potluck luncheon. It's the least I can do to thank them for their willingness to pair up dirty lacrosse boots and find names inside chemistry books. I provide two main courses, because it's easy when I possess the oven. I invented this dish one term because I had a great number of chicken thighs (don't ask, it's a cookbook-writing thing) and nothing exotic to put with them. It is easy to have all these ingredients on hand with nothing unusual to shop for, and the combination of flavors is surprisingly sophisticated. Since the recipe easily doubles and indeed triples, it is perfect for a large group, and can be assembled even the night before, and cooked just when needed.

(serves at least 4)

8 chicken thighs, bone-in, skin on

4 cloves garlic, finely chopped

1 cup/200g black oil-cured olives

1 medium white onion, sliced

¼ cup/60ml each: white wine, olive oil, chicken stock

juice of ½ lemon

plenty of fresh black pepper

4 bay leaves

dozen chestnut mushrooms, sliced

handful capers

1 tbsp cream

Place the chicken thighs skin up in a nice heavy baking dish. Scatter over the garlic, olives and onion. Mix the wine, oil, stock and lemon juice in a small bowl, then pour over the chicken. Sprinkle black pepper on top and tuck the bay leaves in with the onions and garlic. Sprinkle on the mushrooms and capers. Cover the whole thing tightly with foil.

Braise in a medium oven, about 325°F/160°C, for two hours. Remove the foil and up the heat to about 450°F/225°C. Roast in this oven for 30 minutes, or until the skin of the thighs is golden and crisp. Pour the juices and vegetables from the dish into a frying pan (discard the bay leaves) and add a tablespoon or so of cream, whisking to mix. This will be the best gravy you have ever, ever tasted.

sautéed parcels of chicken stuffed with mozzarella, spinach and bacon

This dish is an excuse to gather together some of our family's favorite ingredients and marry them off. There is something delightfully Mediterranean about the combination that makes for a special meal, as well as the bit of fuss it takes to make the parcels. It's a simple assembly job, and the resulting juicy chicken with melted cheese spilling out is a delight.

(serves 4)

4 chicken breast fillets

4 handfuls spinach

4 tbsps pesto

1 ball buffalo mozzarella

16 strips streaky (American) bacon

16 toothpicks

1 tbsp olive oil

1 tbsp butter

Gather your ingredients and ensure they are in easy reach, and get a sharp knife. Lay each chicken breast on a cutting board and carefully cut a pocket horizontally through the breast, not going all the way through to the back.

Spread a spoonful of pesto in each pocket, and tuck the spinach leaves and a quarter of the mozzarella ball into each pocket. As best as possible, close up the pocket and wrap each breast in four strips of bacon, securing the bacon through the chicken with the toothpicks.

Sauté the parcels in a hot frying pan with the olive oil and butter, about 15 minutes, turning frequently, until chicken is cooked through. Just before serving, cut each parcel in half and leave them open in the frying pan, so the cheese oozes out.

chicken burgers with goat cheese and spring onions

Who doesn't love a burger, piled high with all the trimmings: lettuce, onions, cheese, even sautéed mushrooms, pesto and a fried egg? But in this day of trying to eat less red meat, burgers have become a treat. I decided to switch to chicken – ground at home, since I am devoted to my home grinder and use it all the time. We discovered that all of us preferred the texture of ground chicken to ground beef – it is smooth and uniform and completely without fat, and the mild flavour of chicken lends itself to anything you'd like to pile on top.

(serves 4)

4 large chicken breast fillets, skin removed

8oz/225g goat cheese

6 spring onions, green parts only, finely chopped

4 tbsps mayonnaise

fresh black pepper

mozzarella to top burgers: 1 slice per burger

Trim the chicken fillets very well, removing any fat, sinews and the tendon in the tenderloin. Cut into large chunks and either pulse in the food processor or put through a mincer/grinder until medium-fine in texture. Try for the texture of ready-ground beef.

Mix all ingredients except mozzarella in a large bowl. Form into four burgers.

Grill on medium heat (350°F/180°C) for six minutes per side, or until cooked through. Equally, these burgers may be fried in a pan on the stove. In the last two minutes of cooking time, top each burger with a slice of mozzarella.

slow-braised whole chicken with root vegetables

For a family who is not part of the military, ours has moved house a startling number of times. Avery has moved eight times in 17 years. We have become very good at it. One small thing that makes the admittedly disruptive experience more bearable is this dish, really the ultimate in comfort food. I have learned to keep out of the moving cartons a cutting board and good knife, one heavy casserole dish, three plates and cutlery, and three drinking glasses (Scotch-sized, to be sure). I go to the new house in the mid-afternoon of move-in day and put this dish in the oven. When we all arrive late in the day, exhausted and hungry, the aromas of fresh herbs, wine and garlic waft to us from our new oven. Life is a bit of all right, that first night in our new home.

(serves 4 with leftovers)

2 tbsps butter

large stalk rosemary

large stalk thyme

1 whole large chicken, about 4lb/2kg

4 carrots, cut in large chunks

4 stalks celery, cut in large chunks

1 white onion, cut in large chunks

1 large parsnip, cut in large chunks

6 cloves garlic, finely chopped

1 cup/240ml white wine

1 cup/240ml chicken stock

Butter the bottom and sides of a heavy oven-proof casserole with a fitting lid. Place the herbs in the bottom and place the chicken on top, breast-side down. Arrange the vegetable around the chicken and pour over the wine and stock.

Cook in a slow oven (300°F/150°C) for about 3 hours. Because the chicken has cooked breast-side down, it will not have crisp skin, but it will be luscious.

chicken tenders with spicy mayo

When we spend the summers in Connecticut, we all, at some point, long for a dinner of good old-fashioned deep-fried food. Before I acquired a deep-fat fryer of my own, I was content with the food produced by our local joint where you stand in line at a window and place your order with a bored high-school girl. But there was always too much breading on everything I ordered: onion rings, shrimp, and most especially chicken tenders. These are very easy to make and my recipe is much more generous with the meat. Adults will find them nostalgic and yet much better than anything from our childhoods, and children simply devour them.

(serves 4)

6 chicken breasts, completely trimmed
    of fat and sinew

½ cup/60g flour

¼ cup/30g combined seasonings to your
    taste: paprika, garlic powder, basil,
    celery salt, Old Bay Seasoning and of
    course Fox Point Seasoning all make
    good combinations (I often combine
    all these for a truly savory crust)

2 eggs

¼ cup/60ml light cream

2 cups/140g fresh breadcrumbs

enough oil/lard to fill your deep fat fryer

Trim the chicken completely of any fat or membranes. Cut width-wise against the grain in two or three long slices, depending how large the breasts are (you want generously thick slices). Shake up the chicken in the seasoned flour. At this point you can leave the tenders in the fridge while you prepare other dishes.

When you are ready to cook, heat up your oil and at the last minute, shake the tenders one more time to coat thoroughly, then beat the egg and cream in a shallow bowl and dip the tenders in it. Quickly transfer the tenders to the breadcrumbs (also in a shallow bowl) and coat them. Fry for about three minutes.

Serve with 1 cup spicy mayo (see recipe p. 224)

chicken larb on butter/Little Gem lettuce

When we lived in Tribeca, in Lower Manhattan, there was a Thai restaurant through whose doors I never walked, but who delivered this most delectable dish to us on hot summer nights. When we moved away, and I became, gradually, a more inventive cook than my Indiana roots would ever have predicted, I decided to replicate it at home. This is a very good version, and I like it almost equally with shrimp instead of chicken, minced quite small. It is a very refreshing dish, and wrapping it in lettuce makes it a festive thing to bring to a potluck picnic.

(serves 4)

zest of 1 lemon

zest of 1 lime

5 garlic cloves

1-inch piece of ginger, peeled

4 chicken breast fillets, skinless, cut in chunks

1 tbsp olive oil

1 tbsp sesame oil

2 tbsps Thai fish sauce

1 red onion, finely chopped

3 tbsps lime juice

handful cilantro/ coriander, roughly chopped

handful mint, roughly chopped

handful basil leaves, roughly chopped

½ cup chopped mixed nuts or pinenuts

12 leaves butter/Little Gem lettuce

In your food processor, process the zests, garlic and ginger until fine. Add the chicken and pulse into it is just minced, but not mushy.

In a large skillet or wok, heat the oils and sizzle the citrus mixture briefly, then add the chicken. Fry the chicken, constantly chopping and separating it into tiny bits, for 4 minutes, then add the fish sauce. Turn down the heat and let the chicken bubble for a few more minutes, then add the chopped red onion and bubble just briefly, about a minute. Remove to a serving bowl and chill.

Just before you're ready to eat, pour in the lime juice and sprinkle over the herbs and nuts, and toss. Serve in the butter/Little Gem leaves with the cucumber strips.

chicken sausages with feta, red onion and chives

You know the expression, "Legislation is like sausage: no one wants to see how it's made"? A year or so ago in the UK, there was a food nightmare called the "horsemeat scandal." It was discovered in some of the most reputable supermarkets that their ready-formed "beefburgers" were in fact part horsemeat. This scandal expanded to include "beef meatballs" that were in fact part pork, a story destined to raise concerns in the kosher and halal communities. To my mind, just the community of people who eat anything needed to be protected from such duplicity. I have nothing against eating horse or pork, if they are humanely raised, but not if they are called beef. So I began grinding all my own meat (in the UK this is called "mincing"). It was but the work of a moment for this obsession to evolve into making my own sausage. It's a lot of fun for two people to do together, if you're in the mood for a bit of a mess. Furthermore, you DO see how your sausage is made.

(serves 4)

3lb/1.5kg chicken breast fillets, carefully trimmed

2 tbsps Penzey's Fox Point Seasoning (or other savory herb blend)

1 tbsp olive oil

1 large red onion, diced

2 cloves garlic, finely chopped

8oz feta cheese (goat cheese would do as well)

handful chives, finely chopped

casings enough for 3lb chicken (your butcher will know)

butcher's string

Put your chicken through the grinder and set aside in a large bowl. Sprinkle the seasoning over.

Heat the olive oil in a frying pan and fry the onion and garlic until soft. Allow to cool slightly.

Mix the chicken, vegetables, cheese and most of the chives very well (keeping a little bit of chives aside for sprinkling when ready to serve). Take the blade out of your mincer and reassemble with the filler nozzle.

Slide your casings onto your sausage nozzle and tie off the very end. Begin putting the chicken mixture through while shaping the sausages. Fill the entire casing, then twist the long sausage at intervals to form the size you want and tie the whole thing off at both ends. In the same frying pan you used for the onions, with a little more olive oil, sauté the long sausages (made up of small sections) until thoroughly cooked (perhaps 10–12 minutes). Then cut them off at the intervals. Sprinkle with chives and serve with Dijon mustard.

lillian hellman chicken

This dish has a silly name. The recipe is adapted from one on the label of Hellman's mayonnaise, but that didn't seem posh enough, so we named it after the great American playwright Lillian Hellman, author of *The Children's Hour* and many other works. She was romantically involved for many years with novelist Dashiell Hammett, and since we always eat "Lillian Hellman chicken" with cheesy spinach casserole, that dish is named "Dashiell Hammett spinach". While the human relationship was fraught with drama and controversy, the marriage between the chicken and spinach dishes is quite perfect.

(serves 6)

6 chicken breast fillets, well-trimmed

²⁄₃ cup/180ml mayonnaise

1 cup/100g grated parmesan or pecorino

zest and juice of 1 lemon

1 tsp Penzeys Fox Point Seasoning
 or other chicken seasoning

plenty of fresh-ground black pepper

2 cups/140g bread crumbs

Mix the mayonnaise, cheese and lemon juice and zest in a shallow bowl. Place the breadcrumbs in another. Line a large cookie sheet with foil, or use a non-stick baking sheet. Smear each chicken breast, on each side, with the mayonnaise mixture, then roll in breadcrumbs. Place in a single layer on the foil-lined tray. Bake at 400°F/200°C for 25 minutes. Slice thickly and serve hot.

mama nel's buttermilk herbed chicken

When my mother and father were a newlywed couple, they took to calling each other "Mel" and "Nel," for reasons lost in the mists of time (they are named Paul and Suzanne). My father then went a fond step further and called my mother "Mama Nel" once she had children. She was a very reluctant cook, never happy in the kitchen, but this dish was a delicious standby, a sort of homemade version of Shake 'n Bake. I've made the recipe slightly fancier by marinating the chicken in buttermilk, which lends a tart note to the finished dish.

(serves 4)

1 large chicken, or 2 breast fillets and 2 whole legs (split into thigh and drumstick if you like)

2 cup/480ml buttermilk

¼ cup/33g cornstarch/cornflour

¾ cup/100g plain flour

1 tbsp each: dried sage, basil, oregano, garlic powder, onion powder, paprika, celery salt

3 tbsps olive oil

Quarter the chicken if using a whole chicken (reserve the spine for stock). Place the chicken pieces in a large zippered plastic bag and pour in the buttermilk. Squeeze the chicken pieces around in the buttermilk to coat thoroughly and refrigerate for at least 2 hours.

When you are ready to cook, shake the cornstarch, flour and all the dried seasonings in another large zippered plastic bag. One at a time, place the chicken pieces in the bag and shake until thoroughly coated.

Line a large baking dish with foil and pour in the olive oil. Place the chicken pieces skin-side-down in the oil. Bake at 425°F/220°C for 30 minutes, then turn skin-side-up and bake for another 30 minutes.

simple chicken and broccoli stir-fry
with mushroom fried rice

Our family loves an elaborate many-vegetable stir-fry – a sort of catch-all dish when you feel you need an infusion of color and vitamins (see recipe p. 90). But when we found ourselves in Edinburgh on a university visit, in a small flat with empty cupboards, we were reluctant to invest in so many ingredients for one dinner. It became apparent that simplicity can be wonderful. With just a very few ingredients, this dish revived us from our sore feet to our heads filled with dreams of Avery's future.

(serves 6)

6 chicken breast fillets

small bottle (150ml, about ½ cup) oyster sauce

2 tbsps soy sauce, plus extra to serve

6 cloves garlic, finely chopped

2 bunches spring onions, sliced (green parts too)

1-inch piece ginger, peeled and finely chopped

1 large head broccoli, separated into bite-size florets

2 red bell peppers, cut into bite-size chunks

2 tbsps groundnut or vegetable oil

6–8 medium brown mushrooms, diced

4 eggs, beaten

1½ cups/300g basmati rice, steamed

2 tbsps soy sauce, or to taste

handful roasted cashews, roughly chopped (optional)

handful cilantro leaves (optional)

Trim the chicken and slice very thin on the bias, then place in a bowl with the oyster sauce, the first 2 tbsps soy sauce, garlic, one bunch of sliced spring onions, and the ginger. Stir well to coat chicken and leave aside while you prepare everything else.

Stir-fry the chicken until just cooked, then remove to a serving bowl, leaving as much of the sauce behind as possible. In this sauce, cook the broccoli and peppers till they are slightly softened. Add the vegetables to the chicken in the serving bowl, toss till mixed, and cover with a lid or foil to keep hot.

In the same pan, add the oil and stir-fry the mushrooms until just softened. Push the mushrooms to one side and add the beaten eggs to the empty side and scramble. Throw in the steamed rice and stir-fry mushrooms, eggs and rice together, sprinkling with soy sauce. Serve at once with the still-hot chicken and vegetables. Top with the cashews and cilantro, if using.

chicken livers with mushrooms on toast

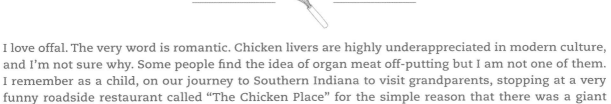

I love offal. The very word is romantic. Chicken livers are highly underappreciated in modern culture, and I'm not sure why. Some people find the idea of organ meat off-putting but I am not one of them. I remember as a child, on our journey to Southern Indiana to visit grandparents, stopping at a very funny roadside restaurant called "The Chicken Place" for the simple reason that there was a giant plastic chicken on top of the roof. This restaurant served everything deep-fried, including chicken livers, and they were a family favourite. This more elegant presentation of livers is simplicity itself, and a rich Sunday-night type of supper.

(serves 4)

2 tbsps butter

1lb/400g chestnut mushrooms

1 banana shallot, finely chopped

3 cloves garlic, finely chopped

2 tbsps Madeira

1 dozen chicken livers, trimmed of all
    fat and sinews

3 tbsps single/light cream

sea salt and fresh black pepper to taste

4 slices sourdough toast

handful chives, chopped fine, to garnish

Melt the butter in a heavy frying pan and fry the mushrooms and shallot until nicely softened. Add garlic and soften as well. Add chicken livers in a single layer, and cook, turning occasionally, until just barely cooked, but still pink inside (the outsides will brown on contact with the hot metal). Add cream and season to taste. Pile onto toast and scatter chives over. Serve hot.

roasted duck on a pancake with plum sauce

One of our favorite Chinese delivery treats in the UK is "Peking" or "crispy" duck: an elaborate preparation involving many exotic spices and dry-hanging, then a very slow roast with much basting. One can also buy improbably bright-red, glazed roasted ducks from hooks in the windows of restaurants in Chinatown. But it is very simple to prepare a roasted duck at home without any fuss. If you cannot find Chinese pancakes where you are, this duck is equally delicious wrapped in large lettuce leaves (butter, Bibb or Little Gem). The fresh, homemade plum sauce is less cloyingly sweet than the bottled sort and adds a lovely richness to the pancake or lettuce parcel. Have plenty of napkins on hand; these parcels are drippy!

(serves 4)

1 large fresh duck (in the UK, I look for Gressingham)

sea salt and fresh black pepper

sprinkle Chinese five-spice blend

2 red peppers, sliced fairly thin

2 small or 1 large cucumber, seeds removed and cut into batons

handful mushrooms, sliced fairly thin

16 Chinese pancakes

plum sauce (see recipe p. 222)

Line a deep-sided ovenproof dish with foil and place the duck in it, breast-side up. Prick the duck all over with a sharp fork or knife. Sprinkle with salt, pepper, and five-spice blend. Roast in a low oven (300°F/150°C) for about two hours.

Shred the duck flesh and skin with two forks and arrange the meat on a platter, along with the vegetables. Everyone can reach for pancakes and make parcels.

roasted guinea fowl with rosemary and 30 cloves of garlic

This dish is inspired by the great British cookery writer Delia Smith, for over 40 years the very best source for tried-and-true recipes for British ingredients. I can't believe I reached nearly the age of 50 before I tasted guinea fowl, but when I saw it in my butcher's glass case, I had a premonition that it would top every roasted chicken I had ever produced. This turned out to be true. The meat is rich and darker than chicken; in fact, the uncooked bird's legs are almost black under the golden skin. Roasted slowly, the finished bird is so tender and juicy that I could hardly believe it is lower in fat than chicken. The meat has a more pronounced flavour than chicken and can easily stand up to this hearty, garlicky treatment. Any leftovers make superb salad, just mixed with celery and mayonnaise.

(serves 4)

1 tbsp butter

good splash olive oil

1 guinea fowl, 4lb/1.8kg, washed, then dried with paper towels

30 cloves garlic

3 stems rosemary

1 cup/250g white wine

3 stems rosemary leaves, chopped fine

sea salt and fresh black pepper

1 tbsp flour

1 tbsp Madeira or Marsala wine

1 tbsp light cream

In a heavy, deep pot with a close-fitting lid, melt the butter and oil together and brown the bird on all sides, turning over with tongs. Remove the fowl to a plate and place the garlic cloves (unpeeled) and rosemary stems in the pot. Place the fowl on top of them, pour over the white wine and sprinkle over the chopped rosemary. Season, then place a double sheet of foil over the pot and clamp the lid down tightly. Roast at 400°F/200°C for an hour, then remove the lid and roast for a further 10 minutes. Let rest for a further 10 minutes before carving.

While the bird is resting, pour the garlicky juices (leaving the garlic itself behind in the pot) into a frying pan and sprinkle with the flour, wine and cream. Whisk over a low heat. Carve the bird.

Serve with the garlic cloves, which can be squished with a fork to release their warm, creamy, soft insides.

herb-brined roasted turkey

Brining is all the rage now in turkey circles, and posh shops sell outrageously-priced herb mixes to aid the nervous cook. These are entirely unnecessary. All that is needed is a simple mixture of inexpensive salt and whatever fresh herbs you like, plus any stray dried herbs you have on hand and would like to use up. The process greatly enhances the tenderness of the meat and allows you to buy an inexpensive frozen turkey that will yield a delicious result, making it a wonderful choice of main course to feed a crowd.

(serves 12 with leftovers)

1 x 13lb/6kg frozen turkey

2 cups inexpensive salt

6 stems fresh rosemary

6 stems fresh thyme

2 tbsps whole black peppercorns

any various dried herbs you have available

3 tbsps butter

Mix the salt with 4 cups boiling water and stir to dissolve completely. Mix with ice cubes to bring the water to room temperature and pour into a stockpot large enough to contain your turkey but that can fit in your refrigerator (in very cold weather, however, the turkey in its brine may be stored, covered tightly, outdoors).

Place the turkey in the brine and add the herbs, then add enough water to cover the turkey completely. It will float. Keep turkey in brine for two days, or until completely thawed.

Place the turkey in a roasting dish and smear the butter over the breast and legs. Cover with aluminum foil and roast at 350F/180C for four hours. Remove foil and roast for a further 30 minutes, then remove from oven and replace foil. Allow the turkey to rest for 30 minutes before carving.

slow-braised beef cheeks with stout and mushrooms 85

beef fillets with duxelles and madeira 86

pierrade of sirloin with satay and plum sauces 89

rump steak stir-fry with many vegetables and sesame fried rice 90

moroccan lamb meatballs with poached eggs in a cumin tomato sauce 93

slow-braised leg of lamb with umami rub and puy lentils 94

rose veal chops with creamy mushroom sauce and fresh sage 96

olimpia's pork spare ribs and meatballs in tomato sauce 97

pork chops steeped in mango, papaya and pineapple with barbecue sauce 99

classic cassoulet 100

honey-roasted ham 105

meats

Our family does not eat a great deal of red meat. We have begun to substitute chicken for many dishes that used to involve beef: Bolognese sauce and burgers, for example. That being said, there are some evenings when the rich, luxurious flavor of beef, pork or veal is very appealing, usually in winter, for us.

Several of these recipes call for beef fillet, which I realize is a pricey option. When you cook fillet, though, there is no waste, and if it appears on your table as a special treat, there's no harm done. My conscience is eased further by the first recipe in this chapter, calling for the cheek of the animal.

slow-braised beef cheeks with stout and mushrooms

I am a firm believer in the "nose to tail" eating philosophy propounded by the British chef Fergus Henderson. If we are going to raise and kill animals for their meat, it's essential that we value every part of the animal that we can. Beef or ox cheeks are a perfect example of this approach; too often thrown away, they are an inexpensive cut of meat that cooked sensitively is as velvety and rich an eating experience as you could wish. Because I cook this dish in the UK, I use stout as the main cooking liquid and flavor, but in the US you could use any dark beer. If you cannot get beef cheeks, beef short ribs may be substituted, but they will not be as rich.

(*serves* 4)

2 beef cheeks, trimmed of top layer of sinew (peel it off in a sheet), but leave other residual fat and membranes as they will cook perfectly)

2 tbsps vegetable oil

1 white onion, diced

6 cloves garlic, finely chopped

2 carrots, diced

6 large-ish mushrooms, quartered or cut in eighths depending on size

2 stalks fresh thyme, leaves only and chopped

1 bottle stout (Guinness)

1 liter chicken or beef stock

Slice the beef cheeks in half to make a portion per person. In a heavy ovenproof dish with a lid, heat the oil and sauté the beef cheeks just briefly on all sides and remove to a dish. In the remaining oil, sauté all vegetables till soft. Add the thyme, cheeks and the stout, then add enough stock for the meat and vegetables to be completely, generously covered. Place in a low oven, 325°F/160°C, covered. Cook for at least four hours.

When the beef is done, remove the cheeks to a warm platter and strain sauce through a sieve into a frying pan. Over high heat, reduce the sauce by about half. Serve beef with noodles or mashed potatoes, and spoon some sauce over. Provide the rest of the sauce in a warm sauceboat at table.

beef fillets with duxelles and madeira

When I was a very young 18, I drove nine hours across Indiana, Illinois and Iowa to spend a week with my boyfriend (now husband) at his family home. His mother, who became one of my closest friends, fed me this dish my first night with them, and I had never tasted anything so sophisticated. The humble mushroom is really elevated here to a meaty accompaniment for the fillet. You will be surprised at both the extent to which the mushrooms cook down, and also your guests' appetites for them, so do not skimp. There are never leftovers.

(serves 4)

4 fillet steaks (or sirloin if you prefer)

4 tbsps butter

2lbs/800g chestnut or Portobello mushrooms, finely chopped

1 banana shallot or three little round shallots, finely chopped

good splash Madeira or Marsala wine

lemon juice and Tabasco to taste

sea salt and fresh black pepper to taste

3 tbsps cream

4 pieces wholemeal bread, crusts cut off

handful flatleaf parsley, leaves only, finely chopped

Bring steaks to room temperature.

Melt butter in a heavy frying pan and fry mushrooms and shallots over a medium heat for 5 minutes, until softened. Add splash of Madeira or Marsala, then fry gently for about 20 minutes, stirring frequently. The mushrooms are finished when they release no more moisture and are quite dry in the frying pan. Turn off heat at this point.

Meanwhile, grill or pan-fry your steaks to your liking, about 3 minutes per side for medium-rare for steaks of average thickness. Let steaks rest while you toast the bread, and reheat the mushrooms.

Place one steak on each piece of toast and divide the mushrooms among them, letting them tumble over the top of the steak. Sprinkle parsley on top and serve right away.

pierrade of sirloin with satay and plum sauces

My friend Annie invited us to dinner in London once, years ago, saying, "It's pierrade." I was no wiser when I heard this word, but she is a great cook so I went along in the spirit of adventure. "Pierrade" is a French way of cooking meat that involves a very hot stone placed in the center of the table with platters of bite-sized raw beef and duck at the elbows of dinner guests. Guests cook the pieces of meat for themselves using very sharp forks, and dip them in a variety of sauces. The French often go one step further in this activity by melting cheese in little dishes under the hot stone and spreading the cheese in slices of baguette. This is called "raclette" and you will probably find that in order to acquire a "pierrade" stone you will end by buying a "raclette" set. With a hearty salad on the side, pierrade is an exciting way to cook dinner, and one of most enjoyable meals to offer guests.

(serves 4)

2 large sirloin steaks

2 large duck breast fillets

1 tsp peanut oil

satay and plum sauces
   (see recipes p. 226 and p. 222)

The key to preparing pierrade is to trim the sirloin and duck completely of any gristle or fat, and to cut the pieces very small and uniform. You may include the duck skin on the pieces if you like, or remove the skin for a leaner dish.

Arrange the meat on platters within reach of all your guests and encourage them to cook their own morsels, then dip them into the sauces.

rump steak stir-fry with many vegetables and sesame fried rice

(serves 4)

4 rump steaks

3 tbsps soy sauce

2 tbsps toasted sesame oil

1 tbsp Mirin (Japanese rice wine)

6 cloves garlic, finely chopped

1-inch piece ginger, peeled and grated

1 tsp Chinese five-spice

1 tbsp peanut oil

2 bunches spring onions, sliced thin, put into two equal piles

2 orange or red bell peppers, cut into chunks

1 small head broccoli, cut into small florets

1 large bunch asparagus, cut into bite-sized pieces

1 large red onion, cut in bite-size chunks

handful sugar snap peas

1 cup/195g basmati rice

2 tbsps peanut oil

1 tbsp sesame seeds

3 eggs, beaten

sprinkle of sesame oil and soy sauce

This is a luxurious take on a family favorite, and quite the best way to get everyone to eat a great many vegetables. The crunchy peppers and broccoli are a good foil for the soft meat, and homemade fried rice is much lighter and more delicious than the restaurant variety.

Cut the beef into bite-sized pieces and place in a small bowl. Add the soy, sesame, mirin, garlic, ginger and Chinese five-spice and stir well. Set aside.

Pour the first tablespoon of peanut oil in a heated wok and cook one pile of spring onions and all the other vegetables, till they are softened to your liking. Set aside in a bowl large enough to eventually hold all the ingredients for this dish.

Steam the basmati rice. Meanwhile, pour beef and its marinade into the hot wok and cook just until done. Place the meat in the large bowl with the vegetables and cover with a pot lid to keep warm.

Pour the remaining two tablespoons of peanut oil into the wok and toast the sesame seeds. Sauté the second pile of spring onions in the oil. Push them to one side; add the eggs and scramble until done. Add the steamed rice and sprinkle on a bit of sesame oil and soy sauce, then toss all together. You may serve the rice separately from the beef and vegetables, or toss them all together.

moroccan lamb meatballs with poached eggs in a cumin tomato sauce

To celebrate a landmark birthday, our friends Vincent and Peter invited the three of us to join them in Marrakech for an extravagant celebration. "You want us to bring along our ten-year-old daughter? To join you guys, and a crowd of your friends at a Riyadh in Morocco?" we asked. Vincent was adamant: Avery was to come along or none of us came. She was petted and included in every possible adventure, and had the time of her life. One sumptuous lunch featured these meatballs, in a sauce so fragrant that I immediately went to one of the famous spice shops with bright pyramid displays and bought a bag of cumin to bring home. This is comfort food at its most exotic, with the poached eggs acting as small surprises in the sauce.

(serves 4)

2lb/1kg lean lamb mince

1 cup/50g Panko (Japanese) breadcrumbs

1 cup/240ml milk, or as much as you
   need to make meatballs

1 tsp ground cumin

sea salt and black pepper

For the sauce:

1 tbsp olive oil

1 tbsp ras el hanout seasoning

1 tsp ground cumin

2 tsps ground turmeric

dash chili powder

6 cloves garlic, finely chopped

½ white onion, finely chopped

4 x 15oz/400g tins whole peeled
   tomatoes

6 eggs

For the meatballs, simply mix all the ingredients together thoroughly and set aside. To make the sauce, heat the olive oil in a very large, shallow ovenproof dish and add all the spices, garlic and onions. Fry gently for 1 minute. Add tomatoes, squeezing them into bits as you put them in the cooking dish. Stir well and simmer for 15 minutes on the hob/stovetop.

Make the meatballs by gently rolling a golf-ball-sized chunk of the meat mixture in your hands – it will be a rather wet, fragile meatball. Drop each gently into the simmering sauce. Cook for five minutes on a gentle simmer, then carefully turn each meatball over.

Simmer for at least 1½ hours. About ten minutes before you are ready to eat, make wells in the sauce surface and crack the eggs in. The dish will be ready when the eggs have poached. The flavors of the yolk and sauce marry very well together.

slow-braised leg of lamb with umami rub and puy lentils

The concept of umami has become firmly entrenched in our cooking lives now: that extra element of "savory." This rub contains every delicious savory thing easily within reach in my kitchen and the flavors all combine perfectly with the mild lamb and soft vegetables. The dish beautifully cooks itself, filling the house with a very homey and tempting aroma, while you busy yourself doing other things.

(serves 6)

1 whole lemon

6 cloves garlic

2 stalks fresh rosemary, leaves picked

2 stalks fresh thyme, leaves picked

2 tbsps capers

4 anchovies in oil

plenty of black pepper

handful flat-leaf parsley, leaves only

1 lamb shoulder, 4lb/1.8kg

4 onions, sliced

6 carrots, cut in large chunks

2 cups/500g prepared Puy lentils

½ cup/120ml white wine

1 cup/240ml chicken or beef stock

1 tbsp flour

Put all the ingredients up to and including the parsley in a food processor – the lemon skin and all – and process until a nice smooth paste. Rub the mixture all over the shoulder of lamb, on both sides.

Arrange onions and carrots in a foil-lined ovenproof dish and scatter the lentils over, then pour over the wine and stock. Lay the lamb in its rub on top of the vegetables and seal with the lid or foil.

Braise slowly at 220°F/120°C for at least four hours. In the last half hour, drain all the cooking liquids from the dish, and separate the fat from the cooking liquids. Discard the fat, then heat the cooking liquids in a frying pan with a tablespoon of flour whisked in, simmering until the gravy is thickened.

The meat will fall off the bone with the help of two forks.

rose veal chops with creamy mushroom sauce and fresh sage

(serves 4)

1 tbsp olive oil

1 tbsp butter

sea salt and fresh black pepper

4 thick rose veal chops

8 leaves sage, chopped

4 cloves garlic, finely chopped

1 banana shallot, finely chopped

12 chestnut or baby portobello
  mushrooms, sliced

1 tbsp flour

1½ cup/375ml beef stock

good splash Madeira or Marsala

½ cup/118ml crème fraîche or sour
  cream

This dish was inspired by the old-fashioned country cooking of Gladys Taber, the food and lifestyle writer who lived across the road from us in our Connecticut home in the decades after the war. It is equally good made with pork chops, but I am happy that in recent years, especially in Europe, veal has come back from its shameful past. In the past decade, efforts have been made to raise these calves' quality of life, including regular exercise, and so the resulting meat is pink, or "rose" as proper veal is called in England.

In a large saucepan, heat the olive oil, butter and salt and pepper until bubbling fast. Place the veal chops in the saucepan over high heat and fry for 2 minutes, then turn over and fry on second side for two minutes. Remove to a plate and keep warm. In the juices in the pan, fry the sage, garlic, shallots and mushrooms until all are soft. Remove everything to the chop plate.

Sprinkle the flour on the juices remaining in the saucepan and fry until bubbling, adding a bit more butter if needed to make a paste. Pour in the beef stock and Madeira or Marsala and bring to a high simmer, whisking until thickened. Add crème fraîche or sour cream and whisk until smooth.

When about ten minutes away from serving, turn up the heat under the sauce until bubbling and place the chops and the mushrooms in the sauce. Cook, moving the chops around, until they are just pink and firm to the touch, perhaps 10 minutes, whisking the sauce as you do so.

olimpia's pork spare ribs and meatballs in tomato sauce

Olimpia is one of the best Italian cooks I know. She and I first cooked together to prepare a business dinner party for guests from the company where she and John worked. I have no doubt that the more normal thing would have been to hire a caterer, but neither of us wanted to do that. We spent a blissful afternoon together, and between us produced a feast to remember, including this traditional dish. We also became very good friends, and whenever she and her husband Tony come to visit us, she brings an aluminum tray filled with these ribs and meatballs. I'm not sure John would let her in the house without them.

(serves 10 easily)

2 tbsps olive oil

24 pork spare ribs

4 cloves garlic, finely chopped

1 small white onion, finely chopped

1 cup/240ml red wine

1 x 14oz/400g can tomato sauce

2 x 14oz/400g cans peeled plum tomatoes

for meatballs:

1½lbs/600g ground pork

3 eggs

2/3 cups/60g breadcrumbs

1 tbsp Italian seasoning

Heat the olive oil in a heavy, very large pot and brown the ribs all over, on all sides. Add garlic, onion and red wine and simmer, uncovered, for 5 minutes. Add tomato sauce and tomatoes, cover the pot and simmer for 3 hours.

Mix meatball ingredients and form into medium balls (about 15), and drop one by one into the tomato sauce, filled with ribs. Cover the pot and simmer for half an hour, at which point the meatballs will be cooked enough for you to stir the pot. Stir it up gently, mixing the ribs and the meatballs.

pork chops steeped in mango, papaya and pineapple with barbecue sauce

My husband is famous for his refusal to countenance eating a dish that combines fruit and meat. So you can imagine my surprise when he announced firstly that he wanted to cook dinner, and secondly that it would be a dish combining pork chops with (gasp) a medley of tropical fruits! Inspired by a recipe by French chef Raymond Blanc, John bought pineapple, mango and papaya, blitzing them in the food processor with abandon. The resulting dish was remarkable for the softness of the pork. I rightly guessed that it was the recipe's claim to scientific processes that attracted John: the enzymes in these particular fruits tenderize the flesh.

(serves 4)

about ½ lb/250g each: mango, papaya, pineapple, peeled, seeded and cut in chunks

1-inch piece ginger, peeled

8 cloves garlic, peeled

5 small red Thai chillis, or to taste

4 stems fresh thyme, leaves only

4 bone-in pork chops

7oz/200g ketchup

1½ tbsps dark brown sugar

2 tbsps Worcestershire sauce

cayenne pepper to taste

large pinch salt

large pinch fresh ground pepper

In a small food processor, pulverize all the ingredients up to the pork chops until smooth as possible. Smother pork chops in marinade and place in zippered plastic bag. Reserve any extra marinade, in a small saucepan. Refrigerate chops for 3 hours, then turn over, massaging plastic bag to coat all meat. Refrigerate a further 3 hours or longer, then remove from refrigerator for 1 hour before cooking the chops.

Pour the leftover marinade from the plastic bag into the saucepan containing the extra marinade. Add all further ingredients. Cook over a low heat, covered, for at least 15 minutes.

Heat grill to 425°F/220°C and place chops on grill, coat first side with barbecue sauce, and grill for 4 minutes, then turn and coat the second side and grill for a further 4 minutes. Repeat the barbecue procedure once more per side, cooking for about 2 minutes each side until done to your desired doneness. Rest for a few minutes, then slice each chop on the bias and serve with the rest of the barbecue sauce.

classic cassoulet

This recipe is for when you want to make a bit of a fuss. It contains many, many ingredients and requires a whole day to prepare. I like to serve it on New Year's Eve at Red Gate Farm when the days are short and dark and a day in the kitchen is welcome. It is also a favourite for my birthday party, since a day in the kitchen expecting friends for dinner is my present to myself. Guests regularly report that they have either never had cassoulet before, or had it once in France and never forgot it. I cook this dish from an original hand-written recipe given to me in France in 1982, when I was 17.

(serves 8)

for the duck confit:

½ cup/120ml olive oil

½ cup/100g duck fat

4 duck legs

coarse sea salt

4 fat garlic cloves, finely chopped

4 bay leaves, broken in half

2 cups/500ml white wine

for the cassoulet:

4 Toulouse sausages, ready-made
  or make your own

12oz/340g belly pork, skinned and diced
  (slab bacon, or ordinary bacon if you
  must)

12oz/340g lamb neck fillet, boneless
  shoulder or rolled breast, diced

1 large onion, chopped roughly

2 large carrots, chopped roughly

In a large frying pan big enough to accommodate the duck, and which has a lid, heat the duck fat until melted. Place the duck legs skin side down in the frying pan, sprinkle with the salt, garlic and bay leaves and pour the white wine around. Place the lid on top and cook at the tiniest simmer possible, for two hours.

Meanwhile, place the sausages in a 425°F/220°C oven and bake for 20 minutes. Set aside to cool.

In a large stovetop- and oven-proof dish that will hold all the ingredients, place the belly pork and heat gently until fat begins to be released, then raise heat and cook, stirring occasionally, until all the fat has been released. Lift the pork onto a plate with a slotted spoon, leaving all the fat behind.

Add the lamb to the pork fat and cook until colored on all sides, then lift out with slotted spoon and set aside with the pork.

continued over page

2 celery sticks, chopped roughly

1 x 15oz/400g can chopped tomatoes

1 tbsp tomato purée

2 heaped tbsp fresh flat leaf parsley, chopped

1 heaped tbsp fresh thyme, chopped

sea salt and pepper

1 cup/250ml white wine

3 x 15oz/400g cans haricot or cannellini beans, drained and rinsed

3½ cups/875ml chicken stock, with more to add later if needed

for the topping:

1 cup/70g fresh breadcrumbs

2 garlic cloves, halved

4 tbsps butter

2 heaped tbsp fresh flat leaf parsley, chopped

1 tbsp fresh thyme, leaves only, chopped

Add the diced vegetables to the pork fat and cook till soft. Tip the plate of cooked pork and lamb back into the dish. Add the tomatoes, tomato purée and herbs, then season with sea salt and pepper to taste.

Add the wine, haricot beans and chicken stock to the dish and bring to the boil. Stir, then lower the heat so the liquid is just simmering. Keep the mixture in the same dish to cook or transfer it to an earthenware dish.

When the duck has cooked for two hours, remove it from the duck-fat/wine and cool to handle. Remove the skin from the duck, then tuck the duck legs into the cassoulet. Set aside the duck-fat/wine mixture.

Peel off the sausage skins, slice the sausagemeat thickly on the diagonal and tuck into the dish.

Cover the dish and bake for 1 hour, stirring once after 30 minutes. Stir, then cook uncovered for a further 1–1½ hours, stirring halfway, until the meat is really tender and the sauce is thickened. Take the dish out of the oven and remove the duck legs. Strip the meat from the bones (it will fall off easily) and return the meat to the dish. Stir and add a little stock and some of the duck-fat sauce, if necessary. Season if necessary, then return to the oven and bake for another 15 minutes until all the meat and beans are very tender.

ajouter alors quelques oignons, carottes, navets.
le tout bien rissolé à la poêle avec un peu de
graisse et une pincée de sucre pour caraméliser
légèrement les légumes

At this point the cassoulet can be refrigerated for up to two days, then reheated to serve.

For the topping, put the breadcrumbs in a food processor. Add the garlic and chop into coarse crumbs. Heat the butter in a large frying pan until sizzling, then stir fry the breadcrumbs and garlic over a moderate to high heat for 7–8 minutes until crisp and golden. Remove from the heat, toss in the herbs and stir to mix, and season well with salt and pepper.

Ladle the cassoulet in generous servings into warm bowls and sprinkle with a bit of topping.

honey-roasted ham

Everyone loves a roasted ham, or as it is called in England, a "gammon joint." For some reason it tastes like a special treat, even though the meat is affordable in both America and the UK. Around our Thanksgiving and Christmas tables, it is always a popular choice, and the leftovers make fine sandwiches.

(serves 4)

6½lb/3kg ham/gammon joint

4 tbsps runny honey

2 tbsps Dijon mustard

Mix the honey and mustard together. Line a baking dish with aluminum foil and place the ham on it, then pour the honey mixture over the ham and cover lightly with more foil. Roast at 350°F/180°C for two hours, then allow the ham to rest for 30 minutes before carving.

seafood

Shellfish feels like a luxury because I associate it with being on holiday: childhood fried shrimp in South Carolina, steamed lobsters fresh from the boat off the coast of Maine.

The British like their crab both white and brown, but I have never acquired the taste for the very strong brown crabmeat, so my recipes here call for just the white. You may certainly use both meats if you like. You will find more seafood recipes in soups (see recipes pp. 28, 32 and 48), pasta (see recipes pp. 173 and 185), and party food (see recipes pp. 194, 201 and 209)

joel's really crabby crabcakes
with spicy mayonnaise

My brother-in-law Joel is a very generous cook and host, and we each have favorite dishes from the other's kitchen. His crabcakes are among my most-requested meals when he cooks for me because they are nearly all crab, except for the bright green and red of onions and peppers. I have many happy memories of summer meals enjoyed at his terrace table, surrounded by family.

(serves 4)

1lb/450g fresh white crabmeat, cooked and picked over

½ cup/80g spring onions, white and green parts both, thinly sliced

1 red bell pepper, finely diced

½ cup/125ml mayonnaise

3 egg yolks, lightly beaten

1½ cup/105g fresh breadcrumbs

½ tsp chili powder

salt and pepper to taste

3 tbsps vegetable oil

(1 more cup/70g breadcrumbs for rolling)

Mix all ingredients but oil, thoroughly. Form into 3-inch diameter cakes, about ¾ inch/2cm thick. Roll in breadcrumbs and place in a single layer on a platter. Refrigerate as long as possible, at least 2 hours (this will keep them from falling apart while cooking). Before frying, firmly squeeze them into shape once again.

Heat oil in a wide, deep skillet and place crabcakes in a single layer. Fry on one side 4 minutes, then turn and fry for another 4 minutes. Drain thoroughly on thick paper towels and serve with spicy mayonnaise (see recipe p. 224).

tuna tartare

I once had a memorable lunch at ABC Kitchen, the Jean-Georges Vongerichten restaurant in the famed department store on Broadway in New York City. With me were my best friend Alyssa and our mutual friend Ivy Baer Sherman, editor of *Vintage* Magazine, a creative tour de force for which I've been fortunate enough to write. At this lunch I ate tuna tartare, and the combination of friendship, the heady feeling of New York energy, and the perfection of this salad have stayed with me in my memory. You must begin with the very best tuna you can buy, from a fishmonger you really trust.

(serves 4)

1½lbs/600g fresh sushi-grade tuna

2 tbsps tiny capers, drained and chopped

4 cornichons, finely chopped

2 tbsps olive oil

juice of 1 lemon

2 tbsps ponzu sauce

sea salt and fresh black pepper to taste

2 handfuls frisée lettuce

1 avocado, sliced and drizzled with lemon juice

extra olive oil for drizzling

Chop the tuna fairly fine, like ground meat. Place in a medium bowl and add the capers, cornichons, olive oil, lemon juice and 1 tbsp of the ponzu sauce. Season the mixture and set aside.

In another bowl, place the frisée and drizzle with remaining ponzu sauce. Mix with your hands. For each serving, place a bit of frisée and some avocado slices on a plate. Divide the tuna mixture into four servings and place each serving in a little ramekin, packing the mixture tightly. Turn ramekin upside down on plate. Drizzle with a bit of olive oil and serve very cold.

deep-fried haddock with tartare sauce

Everyone knows that the national dish of Britain is fish and chips. Fish and chips is, to me, rather like pizza, popcorn and sex: even when it's bad, it's pretty good. But truly great fish and chips is an art form. Many recipes call for a batter that is thick and soft, but I prefer a crunchy crust to my fried fish. I believe that haddock is best for fish and chips because I do not like a tall fish like cod, but certainly if you do, cod would work just fine for this dish. It's very important to take the time to make your own tartare sauce so that your fish has a worthy partner.

(serves 4)

4 fillets skinless haddock

enough flavorless oil, like sunflower, safflower, soybean to fill your fryer to its capacity

½ cup/50g plain flour

½ cup/64g cornstarch

1 cup/70g fresh homemade coarse breadcrumbs

2 tbsps Fox Point Seasoning or other savory seasoning

2 eggs

1 cup/240ml milk

Make sure the fish fillets are completely dried with paper towel. Heat the oil in your fryer to the desired temperature.

Mix dry ingredients in a wide, shallow bowl. Mix eggs and milk in a bowl. Place all fish fillets in the egg mixture. Have a large plate nearby, ready to receive the fillets once battered.

When ready to fry, dip the fish fillets, one by one, into the flour-breadcrumb mixture, then dip quickly again into egg mixture and again into flour-breadcrumb. Place gently into hot oil in ONE layer. Have a large plate nearby again, topped with several layers of paper towel.

Fry for about 4 minutes or until fillets are stiff. Lift carefully onto the paper towel.

Serve hot with tartare sauce (see recipe p. 223).

crustless crab tart with goat cheese and fresh thyme

This tart was crustless by accident. I approached the cooking of dinner far too late one night to make pastry, and my mother-in-law convinced me that we could put all the fillings into a cheesecake tin with a removable bottom. It worked perfectly and was so much simpler than the pastry version, not to mention saving hundreds of calories in butter, that I've come to prefer it this way. The original flavor combination was inspired by a recipe from the great Irish shellfish chef Richard Corrigan in his marvellous cookbook *The Clatter of Forks and Spoons*.

(serves 8)

1 tbsp butter

1 bunch spring onions, thinly sliced

1lb/400g fresh white crabmeat, cooked and picked over

8oz/225g goat cheese, crumbled

2 tsps fresh thyme leaves

1 pint/500ml heavy cream

6 eggs

fresh ground black pepper and sea salt to taste

Butter the bottom and sides of the springform pan. Scatter the scallions on the bottom. Scatter the crabmeat and the goat cheese and thyme leaves over the scallions.

Beat together the cream and eggs and mix in the pepper and salt. Pour over the other ingredients in the tin.

Bake at 325°F/160°C for 20 minutes, then turn heat up to 350°F/180°C for a further 40–45 minutes. Watch carefully and take out just as soon as the filling in the center stops wobbling when touched lightly. Cool slightly or completely before serving.

teriyaki-roasted side of salmon

A side of salmon is festive. Of course for a family dinner you can easily just buy four salmon fillets, but for a party, nothing beats the majesty of a side. And homemade teriyaki sauce is much thicker, more intense and more flavorful than what you can buy in a jar.

(serves 10)

1 side salmon (about 3lb/1½kg)

Make teriyaki sauce (see recipe p. 222). Cool and pour over the salmon fillet, then bake at 425°F/210°C for 20–25 minutes, depending how "done" you like your salmon.

red-cooked szechuan shrimp

This dish is a greatly simplified version of one in a brilliant cookbook given to me by my mother-in-law when I was first keeping house for myself, *Mrs. Chiang's Szechuan Cooking*. Mrs. Chiang favored cooking in instalments with tasks separated, and I have no doubt that this is the authentic way. But I have found that the method below is much quicker and results in a completely delicious dish. So with apologies to time-honored national cookery techniques, here is one our family favorites.

(serves 4)

2lbs/800g raw shrimp, shells on or off as you like

1 tbsp sugar

6 cloves garlic, finely chopped

1-inch/2½cm piece ginger, peeled and grated

a large handful spring onions, white and green parts both, thinly sliced

1 tsp dried crushed red chili peppers

1 egg white, beaten slightly

2 tbsps mirin (Asian cooking wine)

5 tbsps dark soy sauce

pinch of ground cinnamon

If you have chosen shrimp with the shells on, cut their shells with scissors along the back.

Place shrimp in a bowl and cover with all the other ingredients but the peanut oil. Marinate in fridge for at least an hour.

Heat peanut oil in a wok or frying pan until very hot. Toss in shrimp and marinade and cook, stirring constantly, until shrimp turns pink. Serve with steamed brown rice.

紅燒蝦
RED-COOKED SHRIMP (hóngshāo xiā)

The only thing you can be sure of in a recipe is that it contains soy sauce. Each region has its own way of making red-cooked dishes. In Shanghai they are plain and taste of soy sauce, of course, an authentically pr... ...sh is more than ju... ...mp has a d...

potatoes

In my 1970s growing-up, our family's potato offerings at supper came out of Betty Crocker boxes. In those days, the list of ingredients was probably simpler than it is now; filled with unpronounceable preservatives and thickeners. I spent many hours of my childhood wondering how to make these comforting and creamy dishes from scratch, and now when I look at my list of favorite potato recipes, I can see that my dreams have come true.

grandpa jack's grilled potatoes with vidalia onions

My father-in-law confined his cooking to the grill in their beautiful Waterloo, Iowa backyard. Lamb chops were his specialty. I often went to visit my future in-laws as a college student in the summers, and some of my happiest young adult memories are tied up in those hot, golden evenings, with an icy glass of Scotch, the smell of the grill, and John's dad's wise stories. Later when he became a grandfather, everyone's various names for him became coalesced into "Grandpa Jack." These are his potatoes.

(serves 6)

4oz/113g softened butter

6 medium potatoes/1½lb/600g

1 Vidalia (sweet) onion

4 stems fresh thyme, leaves only

fresh black pepper

2 tbsps additional butter

Lay out a very large sheet of heavy duty aluminum foil on the counter and smear soft butter over an inside square about 12 inches wide, leaving plenty of empty space around the edges.

I like to peel the potatoes (John would rather I didn't). You can choose. Then slice them quite thin, to your liking. Slice the onions the same thickness.

Arrange a layer of potatoes on the buttered foil, topping with a layer of onions and a sprinkle of thyme and black pepper. Dot with pieces of butter. Repeat until you run out of ingredients. Bring two edges of the foil together and crimp the edges to make a seam. Crimp the two resulting ends, making a large, flat parcel with one top and two side seams.

Heat your grill (or oven, for that matter) to 425°F/220°C. Place the parcel inside taking great care not to pierce the foil (hence the heavy duty foil). Grill/bake for about 45 minutes or until potatoes are soft – it is a bit of a guessing game. Obviously you cannot check to see if the cooking is going well because it's important not to pierce the foil while cooking.

orlando's straw potatoes in goose fat

This recipe is adapted from my friend Orlando Murrin's *A Table in the Tarn: Living, Eating and Cooking in Southwest France*, a memoir of his time as a hotelier in France. His cakes are quite small and therefore very quickly cooked. Our versions are larger, for a substantial side dish. They are my daughter's most-requested treatment of potatoes and one that friends anticipate hotly when coming to dinner. For Americans, goose fat (or duck) is not a familiar flavor and it tastes extremely luxurious.

(serves 6)

6 medium potatoes, 1½lb/600g
1 shallot, chopped very finely chopped
sea salt and fresh black pepper
3 tbsps goose fat

Peel the potatoes and cut them into very small matchsticks, whether on a mandolin or by hand, first slicing the potatoes very thinly lengthwise, then piling the slices and slicing them very thinly the opposite direction. Set aside until you are about 10 minutes away from wanting to eat.

When ready to cook, you will find that the potatoes have given off a quantity of water. Drain the potatoes thoroughly and squeeze as dry as you can by placing them on a tea-towel – twisting and wringing as much as possible. Mix with the shallots and plenty of seasoning.

Heat the goose fat in a large frying pan and put in 4 handfuls of potato, shaping as rough circles. Moderate the heat if necessary, but after 3–4 minutes they should have started to stick together and the underside to go brown. Turn with a spatula and cook the other side the same way. They will not be very tidy or regular but they will taste delicious.

perfect potatoes dauphinoise with gruyère

Everyone has a favorite dauphinoise recipe and method. Milk or cream? To stir while cooking, or not? Cheese or none? I have tried all these alternatives and can find nothing wrong with any of them, because the combination of dairy and potatoes, bubbling away, is an instant winner. This recipe includes cream for richness, Gruyère because I love it, and no stirring because it is easier just to leave them alone.

(serves 6)

6 medium potatoes/1½lb/600g

1 tbsp butter

pinch onion powder

pinch garlic powder

sea salt and fresh black pepper

2 small shallots or 1 banana shallot, finely diced

1 cup/100g shredded Gruyère

2 cups/480ml cream

2 tbsps butter

Peel the potatoes and slice them thinly or run them through the slicer of a food processor.

Butter an ovenproof dish about 9 inches/22cm square. Layer half the potatoes on the bottom, then sprinkle over minced shallot, onion and garlic powders. Add another layer of potatoes, then mix Gruyère and cream and pour over the potatoes. Dot in four places with the butter. Bake at 425°F/220°C for about an hour, checking to make sure the potatoes are not browning too much and turning down heat slightly if they are. Serve hot.

buttery sage potatoes

As any Italian cook can tell you, butter and sage are natural partners. Simply sizzled together, they make the perfect pasta sauce. The same is true for this potato dish. The sage cooks to a delightful crunch on top of the buttery potatoes, and each portion of the dish may be cut to include a helping of the deep green leaves. The butter sounds like a lot, but the potatoes absorb it, and that is all there is to it.

(serves 4)

6 medium potatoes/1½lb/600g

4oz/113g melted butter

3 cloves garlic, finely chopped

sea salt and pepper

2 tbsps grated Parmesan or Pecorino

8 sage leaves

Using a mandolin or just going carefully by hand, slice the potatoes very thin, as uniformly thin as possible. Place the potatoes in an overlapping single layer in a round pie plate, then pour over a bit of the melted butter. Scatter the garlic over and dust with salt and pepper. Repeat with layers of potato and drizzled butter until you run out of each. Sprinkle with the cheese and arrange the sage leaves in a flower shape in the center.

Bake at 350°F/180°C for about 45 minutes – 1 hour or until potatoes are soft.

becky's cheesy potatoes

My Southern friend Becky was my best companion during the early years of our lives in London. She knew where to find everything, buy everything, and learn everything, and her daughter Anna was my daughter's best friend for three beautiful years before they moved back to the States. When we came back to Connecticut for the summer, after they had moved away, we invited them to stay with us at Red Gate Farm, and one evening Becky offered to make her favourite "cheesy potato" dish for us. "They're great leftovers." We never found out that evening because we ate them all. They are wonderful for potlucks, and a staple at our Thanksgiving and Christmas dinners.

(serves 8)

3lbs/1½kg potatoes

2¼ cups/225g Cheddar or Double Gloucester cheese

3 round shallots or 1 banana shallot, finely chopped

tbsp garlic powder

1 tbsp onion powder

sea salt and pepper

3 cups/720ml cream

Boil potatoes until easily pierced with a fork, then peel when cool. Grate them on the largest side of a coarse grater or food processor and set aside. Grate the cheese on the same side of the grater and set aside.

Lightly oil or nonstick spray a deep glass or pottery casserole dish, perhaps 9 inches in diameter and 5 inches or so high (mine is round, which is an appealing shape). Scatter a layer of grated potatoes on the bottom, then cover with a layer of cheese, a sprinkling of shallot, a sprinkle of garlic powder, and season well. Repeat layering until you have run out of ingredients, ending with cheese. Then pour the cream over the casserole. You want to cover about ⅔ of the potatoes in depth, with cream.

Bake at 350°F/180°C until bubbly and the cheese begins to brown, about 45 minutes, depending on the depth of the casserole.

perfect french fries

In my experience, there can never be enough homemade French Fries, especially because in our kitchen, diners simply gather around and eat the fries, freshly sprinkled with sea salt, as they come out of the deep fryer.

(serves 6)

6 medium potatoes, 1½lb/600g

1 cup/227g lard/drippings

enough vegetable oil to reach the required level in your fryer

sea salt to taste

Run the cut potatoes under running water for a minute to remove starch, then place in enough water to cover and simmer for 20 minutes. Place on a rack and put in the freezer for an hour.

Remove from freezer and fry at 260°F /130°C for 4 minutes. Drain on paper towels and leave till you want to eat.

Just before you want to eat, fry at 375°F /190°C for about 4 minutes (depending on the thickness of the potato pieces) until golden brown. Drain on kitchen paper and salt liberally.

vegetables
& salads

My husband says he could be a vegetarian if it were not for me, and it's true that he will eat any vegetable roasted with a little olive oil. I like roasted vegetables, but I confess that I like them more with a little fuss, a little butter, a little cheese.

Most evenings our vegetables – broccoli, asparagus, red peppers, sugar snap peas, zucchini – are simply sautéed in olive oil, which doesn't make for much of a recipe. The dishes in this chapter are for evenings when your main course is very simple – a roasted chicken or a grilled chop – and welcomes a fancier side dish.

eggplant, chickpea and tomato casserole

This casserole is hearty and rich, and if you liked, you could leave out the cheese and it is a perfect vegan dish.

(serves 8)

4 medium eggplants, cut in ¼ inch slices

½ cup/125ml olive oil (add more if and as needed)

1 x 15oz/400g can chickpeas

2 x 15oz/400g cans whole peeled plum tomatoes

2 medium white onions, sliced thin

6 cloves garlic, finely chopped

3 balls/15 oz/375g buffalo mozzarella cheese, torn into bite-sized pieces

sprinkling Parmesan or Pecorino cheese

sea salt and fresh black pepper

handful chopped flat-leaf parsley

With all eggplants sliced and ready, heat olive oil in a large shallow frying pan. In a series of single layers, fry eggplant slices until soft. Set aside on paper towels.

Fry sliced onions in the leftover oil until soft, then add garlic. Do not burn the garlic.

When all eggplant and onions and garlic are fried, cover the bottom of a 9x13 casserole dish with a layer of eggplant, then spread the onions and garlic over them. Add another layer of eggplant and scatter over half the plum tomatoes, squeezing them into smallish pieces as you take them out of the tin. Add salt and fresh pepper. Add the chickpeas. Add half the cheese, then finish with a layer of eggplant and top with the rest of the tomatoes and scatter the remaining cheese on top. Season sauce to taste and stir in half the parsley.

Cover with foil and bake at 425°F/220°C for 30 minutes. Serve hot or warm with remaining parsley on top.

This dish can also be assembled in the frying pan in which you cook the eggplants. After you've fried all the eggplants, drain the extra olive oil from them back into the skillet and fry the onions and garlic. Place the eggplants back in, along with the tomatoes, chickpeas, salt and pepper and half the parsley. Simply simmer until the tomatoes are cooked, and add cheese and remaining parsley just before you're ready to serve.

stuffed mushrooms

These mushrooms are always the most popular thing at a potluck, and are perfectly delicious as a vegetarian dish. I like them even more when, as I suggest, they contain a bit of white crabmeat.

(serves 4, one mushroom per person)

5 large flat mushrooms (one to chop up for stuffing)

1 tsp olive oil

1 tbsp butter

1 shallot, finely chopped

3 cloves garlic, finely chopped

1 tsp fresh thyme leaves

1 red bell pepper, finely chopped

⅓ cup fresh breadcrumbs

3 tbsps goat cheese

4oz/100g white crabmeat

sea salt and pepper to taste

olive oil to drizzle

Remove the stems from the flat mushrooms and chop them with the extra mushroom. Set aside.

Heat the olive oil in a heavy frying pan and add all the ingredients up to the breadcrumbs. Saute till soft. Mix in a bowl with the breadcrumbs, goat cheese and crab and season to taste. Pile the stuffing mixture onto the flat mushrooms and drizzle with olive oil. Bake at 425°F/200°C for about half an hour, till hot and cooked through.

dashiell hammett spinach

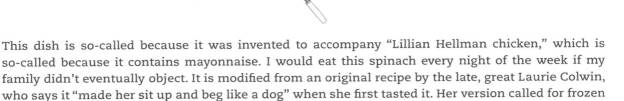

This dish is so-called because it was invented to accompany "Lillian Hellman chicken," which is so-called because it contains mayonnaise. I would eat this spinach every night of the week if my family didn't eventually object. It is modified from an original recipe by the late, great Laurie Colwin, who says it "made her sit up and beg like a dog" when she first tasted it. Her version called for frozen chopped spinach and Monterery Jack cheese, two things not easy to find in London. Now I actually prefer it with fresh spinach as the result is intensely green and fresh. Garlic, cheese and butter? What could go wrong.

(serves 4)

2 tbsps butter

2 tbsps flour

4 cloves garlic, finely chopped

2 tsps celery salt (to taste)

2 tsps celery seeds

1lb baby spinach, washed and spun dry

2oz/60g melting cheese: sharp Cheddar, Fontina, or Edam, shredded (about 1 cup shredded)

2 tbsps cream

1 cup/100g shredded Gruyère

Melt the butter and add the flour in a large frying pan and cook until foamy. Add the garlic and celery salt and saute till soft. The mixture will be rather lumpy and unpromising. Do not despair. Turn off heat.

In batches, put the spinach through the Cuisinart until fairly finely chopped, but not mushy. As you go through the batches, empty each into the frying pan with the buttery mixture.

When all the spinach is in the frying pan, add the shredded cheese and cream and turn on the heat, low. Now simply stir constantly until the cheese is melted and the mixture is thoroughly amalgamated. Pour into a baking dish – about 9x9 will work, or a pie plate – and bake at 425°F/220°C for 20 minutes, till bubbling. If you want a fancier presentation, individual ramekins are pretty.

celeriac remoulade

I bought a little tub of this salad at La Fromagerie in Marylebone, London, for about a million dollars. It was very good, but I thought that I could make it at home in a much greater quantity for very little money, and I was right. Celeriac can be tricky to find in America, and you must ask for "celery root." Or as happened to me in my Connecticut supermarket, "Do you have celeriac?" (Whispered consultation among vegetable men.) "You mean celery root?" "Yes." "Nope." Once you find it, it is a surprisingly versatile vegetable that is at home in all slaws, and makes a marvellous soup, besides this salad.

(serves 6)

1 head celeriac (celery root), peeled

3 tbsps olive oil

1 tbsp mayonnaise

1 tbsp wholegrain mustard

juice of half lemon

Julienne the celeriac by cutting very thin slices and then turning them sideways and cutting those slices into very thin slices. Mix all other ingredients together with a whisk. Toss with the dressing and serve straightaway.

cannellini beans with rosemary, rocket and parmesan

This is one of my husband's most-requested side dishes, inspired by Lynne Rosetto Kasper's *How To Eat Supper*, a very enjoyable cookbook. It can be made rather ascetically with very little oil and cheese, or more luxuriously with greater quantities of both.

(serves 6)

2 tbsps olive oil

2 tbsps butter

6 cloves garlic, finely chopped

2 large stems fresh rosemary, leaves only, finely chopped

2 x 15oz/400g cans cannellini beans, drained

1/3 cup/30g fresh breadcrumbs

1 cup/100g grated Parmesan or Pecorino

2 handfuls arugula/rocket

olive oil to drizzle

fresh black pepper and sea salt to taste

Heat the olive oil and butter in a large frying pan and add the garlic, rosemary and cannellini beans. Saute until garlic is soft. In a clean frying pan, toast the breadcrumbs until crisp and add to the beans. When ready to serve, add the cheese and arugula and toss well. Add more olive oil if needed and season to taste. Serve warm.

roasted beets with balsamic reduction and parsley

I was raised on something called "pickled beets" which came in a jar. For special occasions, my dad would spring for the kind that were "crinkle-cut." This now seems like an odd vegetable for a rather bland Indiana household to enjoy, but I grew up loving them and was amazed as an adult to find that that they came raw, in the vegetable section of the grocery store! While I would not call my grownup version "pickled" as they sit in the vinegar just for the amount of time it takes to cook dinner, they are just as tasty and even more brightly colored than the beets of my childhood. Those who share my enthusiasm for beets will also appreciate a poster I saw in an English greengrocer: "Keep Calm. You Had Beets For Lunch."

(serves 4)

4 medium or 8 small beets
½ cup balsamic vinegar
2 tbsps light brown sugar
large handful flat-leaf parsley

Wrap the beetroots in heavy aluminium foil and roast at 425°F/220°C for at least an hour (for small beets) and as much as two hours (for very large). Leave in foil for about 30 minutes, then open the parcel and peel beets, and cut into bite-size pieces.

Place balsamic vinegar and sugar in a small saucepan and simmer until reduced by half, about 30–40 minutes.

Tear only the leaves from the parsley stems and chop roughly.

Sprinkle the parsley over the beets and drizzle with the balsamic reduction.

butternut squash puree with cayenne and nutmeg

This puree is a beautifully bright side dish to any roasted fowl or grilled chop. Mixed with milk and warmed through, it is a fine soup. Mixed with feta or goat cheese, crisped sage leaves and toasted pine nuts, it is a good vegetarian option for a main course. In short, it is a good puree.

(serves 4)

1 large butternut squash

drizzle olive oil

1 tbsp butter

fresh black pepper to taste

sea salt to taste

3 tbsps half-fat crème fraîche
   or sour cream

1 tbsp light cream

good splash milk

grated nutmeg to taste

chili powder to taste

Line a baking dish with foil. Cut the butternut squash in half lengthwise (do this very carefully as the squash will rock and roll as you split it with the knife). Scoop out the seeds from each half and discard. Sprinkle with olive oil, divide the butter between the halves and place in the seed hollow, and season. Roast at 425°F/220°C for about an hour or until completely soft and browned.

Scoop the softened flesh from the skin and place in a large bowl. Add all the rest of the ingredients and blend with a hand blender. The mixture will not move because of its thickness, so simply move the blender around until all the squash is pureed. Mix well with a spatula.

three-bean, red pepper, sugar snap and corn salad

My across-the-road-neighbor Anne tells me that everyone should eat a portion of beans every day, in soup if it makes them more "palatable." When I gave her a bowl of this bean salad, we agreed there was no more palatable way, indeed delicious way, to offer beans. The bright colors of the other vegetables in the salad are beautiful to look at, and the lemony garlic makes a perfect, light dressing.

(serves 6)

1 x 15oz/400g can black beans, rinsed and drained

1 x 15oz/400g borlotti beans, rinsed and drained

1 x 15oz/400g haricots (small white beans), rinsed and drained

2 ears raw corn, kernels cut off (about ½ cup/200g)

handful sugar snap peas, sliced into quarters

1 red, orange or yellow pepper, diced

1 bunch spring onions, sliced thin, both white and green parts

handful chives, finely chopped

2 cloves garlic

juice of 1 lemon

1 tsp salt

zest of 1 lemon

fresh black pepper to taste

½ tsp crushed red pepper flakes

½ cup olive oil

Mix all ingredients up to garlic, in a large bowl. Place garlic, lemon juice and salt on a cutting board and mince them together; this process pulverizes the garlic to a fine puree and also softens the impact of the garlic, while allowing all the flavour to come through.

Add the garlic to the salad and sprinkle with lemon zest, red and black peppers and olive oil. Mix well.

white cabbage, fennel and carrot slaw
with poppy seed dressing

Anyone who was raised in America is familiar with the slaw to be found in delicatessen windows. It is pale and heavy with far too much dressing, and tasteless. Yet we all eat it, when it is offered to us in a fluted paper cup alongside a sandwich in a diner. This slaw is everything that slaw should be: crisp, colourful and just barely dressed, with a fine poppy seed crunch.

(serves 6)

½ head white cabbage, outer leaves removed, chopped to your liking

3 carrots, grated

2 bulbs fennel, outer leaf removed, chopped fine

Toss well with poppy seed dressing (see recipe p. 225).

tomato and mozzarella salad with pine nuts and basil-avocado pesto

In all the lunch parties I have given, or potlucks to which I've brought this salad, there is never enough. I wonder how much I would have to make in order to have leftovers. The best version is to be made in deepest August in Connecticut when the tomatoes are crowding each other off the tables at the farmers market, alongside huge bunches of basil. The wild card is always the avocado, for which there seem to be several days when they're too hard, about five minutes when they're just right, and then they're too soft. Find those five minutes and make this salad.

(serves 4)

4 large tomatoes

1 large ball buffalo mozzarella

3 tbsps pine nuts, lightly toasted

1 ripe avocado

large handful basil leaves

1 tbsp Dijon mustard

about ½ cup/118ml olive oil, or enough
   to emulsify

juice of 1 lemon

¼ cup/25g grated parmesan or pecorino

sea salt and black pepper to taste

more olive oil to drizzle, if desired.

Cut the tomatoes into bite-size pieces and arrange them on a pretty plate. I find that buffalo mozzarella is nicest to eat when it's been torn, not cut, so tear it up and place pieces between the tomatoes. Scatter the pine nuts over top.

Put all the rest of the ingredients in a small food processor and pulse until the texture you want, able to be spooned over the salad. Drizzle a bit of extra oil on top, if you like.

scallop, roasted beet, goat cheese and spinach salad with avocado and anchovy-mint dressing

This could be called a "superfood" salad if I didn't find that word irritating. It is certainly full of superb flavors and textures, and is a very satisfying whole lunch for a special occasion. I first tasted anchovy-mint dressing in our London neighborhood of Barnes, at a restaurant called "Riva" which specialises in Northern Italian dishes. The combination sounds odd, but you will find it intensely savory and delicious.

(serves 4)

2 tsps butter

12 large scallops

4 medium beets, roasted

large handful baby spinach leaves

8oz/225g goat cheese

8oz/225g bacon, cut into
    small lardons

Heat butter in a heavy frying pan and cook scallops JUST until done, about 1 minute on each side, maybe more if they are very large. Set aside. Cut beets into bite-size pieces, set aside.

Line a large serving platter with spinach and scatter goats cheese over. Fry bacon until it is crisp and has given up its fat. Drain. Place all ingredients on the spinach. Drizzle with anchovy-mint dressing (see recipe p. 225).

cucumber and dill salad

I like this salad best with small cucumbers, either hydroponically grown or best of all, the slender Lebanese ones from our greengrocer Green Valley, off the Edgware Road in London. Small cucumbers are nearly seedless, which is helpful because some people cannot eat cucumber seeds happily. If the only cucumbers you can get are the big waxed monsters, that will be fine if you peel them, cut them in half lengthwise, then scoop out the seeds with a spoon.

(serves 4)

4 small or 2 large cucumbers

handful dill, chopped roughly

1 stalk lemongrass, finely chopped

½ cup/50ml sour cream

juice of 1 lemon

sea salt and fresh black pepper to taste

Cut cucumbers in half lengthwise and slice just as thin as you like them. Place them in a bowl big enough for tossing them around, and sprinkle with dill.

Place sour cream, lemon and seasonings in a small bowl and whisk until mixed. Pour over the cucumbers and toss until mixed.

warm chickpea salad with feta and spinach

I love chickpeas in any form: in tuna salad, in bean salad (see recipe p. 150), in eggplant casserole (see recipe p. 137), in houmous. This salad presents them very simply, and pleasantly warm. The turmeric in the curry powder adds a lovely smoke and golden color, and the feta melts slightly. You could easily substitute goat cheese if you like, or gorgonzola if you want a stronger flavor.

(serves 4)

2 tbsps olive oil

4 cloves garlic, finely chopped

1 small red chili pepper, or to taste, chopped fine

½ medium red onion, finely chopped

2 tsps mild curry powder

2 x 15oz/400g cans chickpeas, drained and rinsed

juice of 1 lemon

2oz/100g feta cheese, crumbled into bite-size pieces

2oz/55g baby spinach, sliced into ribbons

sea salt and fresh black pepper to taste

Heat the olive oil in a heavy skillet or saucepan and fry the garlic, chili and onion gently till soft. Add the curry powder and cook for another minute, taking care not to burn the garlic. It is essential to cook the curry to avoid the bitterness that can come from merely adding it raw to the dish.

Add the chickpeas and the lemon juice and more olive oil if the mixture seems too dry, and cook very gently for about 10 minutes, stirring frequently. Add the feta cheese and toss well till the cheese is warmed. Add the spinach and stir until it is wilted. Season and serve hot or warm.

caramelized carrots

I know it sounds absolutely mad to feed people a pound of carrots each, but trust me when I say that they cook down astonishingly, and also that they are addictive. What could be better than sweet carrots in sweet butter?

(serves 4)

4lbs/2kg carrots

⅓ cup/85g butter

¼ cup/50g brown sugar

Peel and slice the carrots. Melt the butter and sugar in a heavy-bottomed frying pan. Add the carrots and sauté slowly over a low heat, stirring frequently, until the carrots begin to brown, about 20 minutes. Brown to your liking and serve hot or warm.

green beans with garlic and lemon

These are the perfect vegetable to make in large quantities for big gatherings of family and friends. They are appealingly bright green, absolutely everyone likes them, and the lemon zest and garlic elevate them from just plain green beans.

(serves 4)

4 cups/12oz/360g green beans

1 tsp olive oil

1 tbsp butter

4 cloves garlic, finely chopped

zest of 2 lemons

juice of 1 lemon

sea salt and fresh black pepper

Steam the green beans for about 3 minutes, until bright green and the tenderness that you like. Plunge them into a bath of icy water to stop them cooking, then drain and set aside.

In a frying pan, melt the oil and butter together, then gently cook the garlic till soft. Do not allow the garlic to burn. Add the lemon zest and juice, and tip in the green beans. Season to taste and toss until the beans are just warmed through.

four-cheese lasagna with chicken ragu 169

conchiglie and taleggio 170

scallops and two parsleys with linguini 173

spaghetti bolognese with chicken ragu 174

spaghetti carbonara with asparagus and chicken 177

farfalle with broccoli 178

farfalle with spinach and roasted red peppers 181

spaghetti puttanesca 182

spaghetti with clams, garlic, tomatoes and oil-cured olives 185

everything homemade pizza 186

pasta & pizza

Our daughter would eat pasta every night if she had her way.
I have become a little less obsessed with pasta since I had
a six-month wheat-free experiment a year ago, but we have
favorites that we return to again and again. I love pasta as a
vehicle for delivering big flavors, especially with cheeses and
combinations of vegetables. These dishes are my twists on
some classics, and also some inventions of my own.

four-cheese lasagna with chicken ragu

This is a dish I serve to large groups because all children and adults like it. I used to make my lasagna with a mixture of Italian sausage and beef, but now I make it with chicken breast and we all prefer it. It is with this healthful decision that I justify the generous amount and variety of cheese in the dish.

(serves 8)

12 sheets lasagna noodles

2 tbsps olive oil

1lb/400g ground chicken

6 cloves garlic, finely chopped

2 shallots, finely chopped

2 x 15oz/400g can peeled plum tomatoes

dash red wine

2 tbsp Italian seasoning

4 tbsps butter

2 tbsps flour

1 pint/500ml whole milk

8oz/225g ricotta cheese

8oz/225g mascarpone cheese

sprinkle nutmeg

sea salt and fresh-ground black pepper to taste

1 cup/100g grated Pecorino or Parmesan

1 large ball buffalo mozzarella, shredded

handful basil leaves, shredded

Boil the lasagna noodles till cooked, then drain them and brush them with olive oil, in a single layer, to keep them from sticking together.

Heat the olive oil in a large skillet and cook the chicken mince, then throw in the garlic and shallots and fry until they are softened. Add the tomatoes and Italian seasoning and wine and simmer for about 15 minutes, till the sauce is not liquidy.

Meanwhile, melt the butter and add the flour; cook together until bubbling but before it begins to brown. Whisk in the milk slowly, and cook until the mixture begins to thicken, then add the ricotta, mascarpone, nutmeg, salt and pepper and stir until thoroughly mixed.

Ladle just enough of the chicken and tomato sauce into a 9x13 inch/ 23x33 cm glass dish to cover the bottom. Place 4 lasagna sheets on top of the sauce. Pour over half the white sauce. Lay down another layer of noodles and another layer of meat sauce. Sprinkle with the grated Pecorino or Parmesan. Finish with the last 4 lasagna sheets, the last of the meat sauce and pour over the rest of the white sauce. Sprinkle the mozzarella over all, and top with the basil leaves.

Bake at 300°F/150°C for about 45 minutes–1 hour until the lasagna is bubbling and the top beginning to brown.

conchiglie and taleggio

When my friend Alyssa had had her baby Elliot very early and we were all rather worried about them both, I brought to her family a dish of macaroni and cheese, along with a roasted chicken and a chocolate cake, to comfort the family. Her mother held me tearfully in her arms and thanked me, saying, "You are like a daughter to me, like a sister to Alyssa. We can't thank you enough. And darling, really too much nutmeg in the macaroni and cheese."

I have tried many recipes, but this is my favorite. The shells really hold the sauce, and while hard cheese like Cheddar, Double Gloucester and the like yield a pretty orange sauce, it is often a bit grainy, a bit split. This sauce is perfectly creamy. I prefer conchiglie, a shell-shaped pasta, for their ability to hold the sauce. And darling, go easy on the nutmeg.

(serves about 8)

1½lb/600g conchiglie or macaroni

3 tbsps butter

2 tbsps flour

2 pints/1 liter whole milk

1½lb/600g taleggio cheese, without rind

dash fresh-ground nutmeg

tiny dash cayenne pepper

sea salt and black pepper to taste

½ cup/35g fresh breadcrumbs

3 tbsps melted butter

Cook the pasta and spread it into a large buttered dish, large enough to easily accommodate all the pasta and sauce.

Melt the butter in a heavy saucepan and add the flour, cooking together for a bubbling minute or so. Whisk in the whole milk, whisking constantly until sauce is thickened.

Add the taleggio and season with the nutmeg, cayenne, salt and pepper. Stir constantly over a low heat until the cheese is melted.

When the sauce is thoroughly melted and creamy, pour it over the cooked pasta and stir carefully so that all the holes in the pasta receive the sauce. Top with breadcrumbs and drizzle with melted butter. Bake at 350°F/180°C for about 45 minutes, or until the middle of the dish is hot through.

scallops and two parsleys with linguini

This is one of the first recipes given to me by my mother-in-law, a gifted Italian cook, about 30 years ago. It sounds like a lot of olive oil, but then you must consider that it's all the sauce the dish contains. The most important thing is not to overcook the scallops, and not to burn the breadcrumbs as you toast them. There cannot be too much garlic or parsley in this dish.

(serves 4)

16 large sea scallops

1lb/400g linguini

⅓ cup olive oil

5 cloves garlic, finely chopped

½ tsp red pepper flakes

salt and pepper

1 large handful flat-leaf parsley, leaves only, finely chopped

1 large handful curly parsley, leaves only, finely chopped

1 cup/70g fresh breadcrumbs, toasted lightly

The sauce will cook in just the time your linguini needs to boil, so bring the water to a boil and put in the pasta.

In a large frying pan, heat the olive oil and simmer the garlic, but don't let it brown. Place the scallops in the oil and cook on high heat until they turn opaque (about a minute for bay scallops, two minutes for sea scallops), turning occasionally. Add the parsleys, the chili flakes and salt and pepper, and toss gently. Turn off the heat.

Drain the pasta and add to the scallops, then turn up the heat quite high and toss with the breadcrumbs.

spaghetti bolognese with chicken ragu

In Britain, "spag bol" is a thing that lingers with a mixture of nostalgia and horror in people's memories, having appeared on school lunch trays and hospital menus and in cans on grocery shelves. It is a travesty of everyone's favourite pasta dish, "spaghetti Bolognese," traditionally made in Bologna with tagliatelle instead of spaghetti, lots of meat and very little tomato. My version is just slightly tomatoey as well, replaces beef with chicken, and contains a great deal of "soffrito," that onion-celery-carrot mixture that forms the basis of much Italian cooking. The white wine and milk combine to make a delicious sauce.

(serves 6)

1lb/400g angel hair pasta

1 tbsp olive oil

4 cloves garlic, finely chopped

1 white onion, finely chopped

3 stalks celery, finely chopped

3 medium carrots, finely chopped

8 large mushrooms, finely chopped

1lb/400g ground chicken

½ cup/120ml white wine

½ cup/120ml whole milk

2 x 15oz/400g can whole peeled plum tomatoes

pinch ground nutmeg

½ cup/50g grated Parmesan or Pecorino

sea salt and fresh black pepper to taste

extra grated cheese to serve

Heat the oil in a large saucepan with a heavy bottom and add the vegetables, cook until softened. Add chicken and stir over high heat, until just cooked through.

Add the white wine, stir and cook for five minutes. Add the milk, still with heat high. Stir and cook for five minutes. Add the tomatoes, breaking them up with your hands as you do so. Turn down the heat and cook for at least 1 hour, stirring occasionally.

When nearly ready to serve, boil pasta and drain. Shortly before serving, add nutmeg and cheese and stir thoroughly. Season to taste. Toss with boiled angel hair pasta and plenty of extra grated cheese to sprinkle.

spaghetti carbonara with asparagus and chicken

I know that real carbonara sauce does not contain cream, and I have friends who swear by their authentic versions with just egg yolk and the pasta water. Nevertheless, I brought up my daughter eating a creamy carbonara sauce and there is no going back. To ease my conscience, I add asparagus for color and chicken for protein. So really, this is not in any way "spaghetti carbonara." But if you came to my house for dinner, that is what we would call this dish, and it is very good.

(serves 6)

1lb/400g bacon (American or English), diced

½ small white onion, finely chopped

1 bunch asparagus

2 chicken breast fillets

4 cloves garlic, finely chopped

½ cup/125ml cream

½ cup/125ml crème fraîche

1 egg yolk

pinch fresh grated nutmeg

fresh black pepper

1lb/400g spaghetti

½ cup/50g grated Parmesan or Pecorino

Boil water for pasta. Then in a large skillet, sauté bacon over low to medium heat, stirring nearly constantly and taking care that the bacon does not scorch. If you are using American bacon, you will need to drain the fat frequently. British bacon will provide just enough fat for the sauce. When bacon is cooked, add onion, asparagus and chicken and fry until chicken is JUST cooked through, then add garlic, stirring for a moment, then turn off heat.

In a medium bowl, combine cream, crème fraîche, egg yolk, nutmeg and pepper.

Cook pasta and drain, reserving about ¼ cup of the pasta water. Whisk hot water into creamy sauce, then throw the pasta into the sauce skillet and toss well with the sauce and reserved hot water. Serve immediately with cheese sprinkled on top.

farfalle with broccoli

This incredibly simple dish came about one day when the only fresh thing I had in the house was broccoli, and there was a hungry small child to feed. I thought that a pink sauce would be tempting, but without any cream, how could it be achieved? It turns out that tomatoes and pine nuts together make a creamy pink sauce, very appealing to eat. My daughter would eat (and probably will when it's her choice) this dish twice a week. If you happen to have a little goat cheese or Boursin on hand, you can add that to the tomato sauce as you're blending it and it will be that much richer.

(serves 6)

1lb/400g farfalle

1 tsp butter

1 tbsp olive oil

5 cloves garlic, finely chopped

1 white onion, finely chopped

1 tbsp Italian seasoning

6 tbsps/6oz/168g pine nuts

1 x 15oz/400g can whole peeled plum
   tomatoes

1lb/400g broccoli florets

½ cup/50g grated Parmesan or Pecorino

Put water on to boil for the pasta. It will need to cook for about 12 minutes.

Heat butter and olive oil in a shallow skillet and cook garlic and onion till soft, then add Italian seasoning and mix well. Set aside while in a food processor or blender you mix the pinenuts and tomatoes till completely blended and a pleasing sort of reddish pink. Pour the mixture into the skillet with the garlic and onion and heat until bubbling, then turn off heat.

Steam the broccoli and pour into the sauce. Drain boiled pasta and drop into sauce, then toss and serve with grated cheese.

farfalle with spinach and roasted red peppers

This flavor combination was suggested to me in one of the first cookbooks I ever read, *Italian Light Cooking* by Elisa Celli, a gift from my mother-in-law. As usual, I have altered the recipe to suit our tastes, namely adding a much greater quantity of garlic and and larger proportion of vegetables to pasta. It is a top-ten recipe in our household.

(serves 6)

1lb/400g farfalle

5 red bell peppers

4 handfuls spinach

2 tbsps olive oil

5 cloves garlic, finely chopped

1 red onion, finely chopped

2 tbsps Italian seasoning

sprinkle hot red pepper flakes

1 x 15oz/400g can whole peeled plum tomatoes

1 handful flat-leaf parsley, finely chopped

½ cup/50g grated Parmesan or Pecorino

Roast peppers by cutting them in half and laying them skin-side up on a foil-lined cookie sheet, then placing them under the broiler function of the oven for about 10 minutes, until skin is beginning to darken and shrivel. Fold up peppers right in the foil and leave for a few minutes to steam the skins off. Peel and cut in slivers; set aside.

Chop the spinach into slivers; set aside.

Heat the olive oil in a frying pan and sauté the garlic and onion till soft, then throw in the Italian seasoning and pepper flakes and add the red pepper slivers. Add the tomatoes to the sauce by squeezing them each with your hands.

Toss the spinach and parsley in at the last minute and stir till warm, then throw in the pasta and toss all together. Serve with the grated cheese.

spaghetti puttanesca

The legend goes that this sauce was one favored by prostitutes in Italy because all the ingredients could be found in the cupboard with no need to shop, leaving the ladies more time for their professional activities. Whatever the truth of this legend, the flavors in this dish simply sing with salty complexity. Don't be put off by the quantity of anchovies, as they melt away into the sauce, leaving only a perfect savoriness.

(serves 4)

1lb/400g spaghetti

3 tbsps olive oil

4 cloves garlic, finely chopped

7oz/200g oil-cured black olives, pitted and halved

1 x 15oz/400g can whole peeled plum tomatoes

3 tbsps capers, rinsed if held in salt

6 anchovies, rinsed

½ cup/50g grated Parmesan or Pecorino

Boil spaghetti. In the meantime, chop the garlic and onion. Sauté them gently in olive oil in a saucepan, and when the garlic is soft, add the olives, tomatoes (squeezing them into pieces as you go), capers and anchovies. Sauté till mixed. Throw in the drained spaghetti and serve with cheese.

spaghetti with clams, garlic, tomatoes and oil-cured olives

The classic Mediterranean flavors of this sauce are indescribably delicious. In England or France the clams best suited to this dish are Palourde, where in America you will want to look for Littleneck clams.

(serves 4)

1½kg/3½lb small clams, raw

50ml/¼ cup very good quality extra virgin olive oil

6 cloves garlic, finely chopped

3 tbsps butter

2 large handfuls flat-leaf parsley, finely chopped

1 hot Thai chili, seeds removed and finely chopped (or to taste)

fresh black pepper, sea salt to taste

12 cherry tomatoes, quartered

12 oil-cured Moroccan black olives, pitted and halved

1lb/400g spaghetti

2 tbsp olive oil

75ml/6oz good white wine

Clean the clams carefully and discard any that are not firmly closed, or do not promptly close when you tap on them with a fingernail.

In a small frying pan, heat the olive oil and sweat the garlic gently in it. Do not brown the garlic. Add the butter, half the parsley and the chili, the pepper and salt, tomatoes and olives and heat gently until butter is melted.

Just before you are ready to serve, boil the spaghetti until very slightly undercooked, then drain into a serving bowl and toss with the olive oil to stop pasta from sticking.

To the hot, empty pasta pan, pour in the white wine and bring quickly to a boil. Tip in the clams and put the spaghetti in on top. Clap a tight lid on and cook, stirring twice, for 5 minutes.

Pour the clams and spaghetti into the serving bowl and pour the garlic mixture over top, then toss well till completely mixed. Serve with good crusty bread if desired, and discard any clams that have not opened.

everything homemade pizza

I am famous in our house for agreeing to order in pizza, or bringing a pizza home from the grocery store, and then piling it with so many extra ingredients as to render the original pizza null and void. Then I complain about the quality of the crust. I have nearly stopped doing this (although ordering out pizza is something a former New Yorker really has to do, maybe once a quarter).

This dough needs no rising, although it is happy to, so there is no reason at all not to make your own pizza. Then you can pile it with everything but the kitchen sink and rejoice in the flavors you want, plus a perfectly crisp and flavorful crust. The sauce is perfectly simple, too, and doesn't require cooking.

(serves 4, makes 2 pizzas)

For the dough
4 cups/500g plain flour
1 packet/2 tsps dried yeast granules
1 tbsp Italian seasoning
1 tsp each: onion powder, garlic powder
1 cup/250ml warm water
1 tsp olive oil
1 tsp milk
extra flour for rolling out

Get your oven as hot as it will go, and leave it for at least 15 minutes. If you have pizza stones, heat them in the oven as well.

In a large bowl, stir together the dry ingredients until well-mixed. Pour in the wet ingredients and with a fork, stir until slightly mixed, then use your hands to push and pull the dough, scraping the sides of the bowl, until no more flour sticks to the bowl and all has been incorporated. Pizza dough responds to all atmospheric conditions, so simply add more flour or water as needed to make workable dough. Keep kneading in the bowl, adding flour if you need it. Divide the dough in half and roll out with a rolling pin or a clean wine bottle, to the size you like.

Place the crusts on your pizza stones or round cookie sheets and bake for about 10 minutes, or until crisp. If they puff up while baking, just pierce them with a fork when the come out and slap them down.

continued over page

for the sauce:

1 x 15oz/400g can whole peeled plum
tomatoes

handful basil

1 tsp each: garlic salt, garlic powder,
onion powder

suggested toppings:

oil-cured olives

green olives with pimentos

red onion, sliced thin (or sautéed until
caramelized)

red peppers, sliced thin

mushrooms, sliced thin

mozzarella, shredded

goat cheese, crumbled

sausages, pepperoni, chorizo, cooked
through

fresh basil leaves

fresh spinach leaves

pesto

rocket/arugula

crushed red chili flakes

Place all sauce ingredients in food processor and whiz until tomatoes are as smooth as you want them.

Ladle sauce on the crusts, then add desired toppings. Bake the pizzas for about 10 minutes, or until any cheese has melted.

We like to put fresh arugula/rocket on our pizzas after they come out of the oven, along with some hot chili flakes.

party food

I really enjoy a large gathering, when everyone comes hungry and prepared to have a good time. These occasions in London include my Lost Property volunteers' luncheons and various bell-ringers' meetings, both of which are potlucks and very convivial. Probably my favorite party is my mother's birthday every August at Red Gate Farm, with lots of family and friends, the sprinkler going and plenty of children on the trampoline. Having a big long picnic table groaning with food under the dappled summer sun, with my mother's favorite yellow balloons drifting from the hydrangea tree, is close to heaven.

Other recipes in this book that lend themselves particularly well to parties are eggplant, chickpea and tomato casserole (see recipe p. 137), stuffed mushrooms (see recipe p. 138) and a side of roasted salmon with teriyaki sauce (see recipe p. 117).

devilled eggs

Quite simply my mother's favorite food. The curry makes all the difference.

(serves 12)

1 dozen eggs
½ cup/125ml mayonnaise
2 tsps Dijon mustard
1 tsp curry powder
sea salt and fresh black pepper to taste
paprika to sprinkle

Place eggs in cold water in a saucepan in a single layer (two batches if necessary). Bring to a strong boil, then cover and leave for 10 minutes. Peel and cut in half.

Scoop or squeeze out yolks into a small bowl and mash with a fork. Mix in everything else but paprika and stuff each egg half with a spoonful of yolk mixture.

Sprinkle with paprika and keep very cold until serving.

angels on horseback

Get the biggest, most robust scallops you can find for this dish.

(serves 12)

2 dozen sea scallops, muscle removed

2 dozen strips bacon (streaky if in UK)

4 long bamboo skewers

Rinse and pat dry the scallops. Wrap each in a slice of bacon.

Soak the skewers in water for 15 minutes, then thread the wrapped scallops, lengthwise through both scallop and bacon, along the skewers.

Grill on high heat, 425°F/220°C, for about five minutes, turning frequently.

stuffed heirloom zucchini

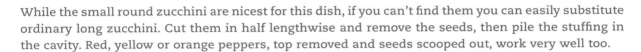

While the small round zucchini are nicest for this dish, if you can't find them you can easily substitute ordinary long zucchini. Cut them in half lengthwise and remove the seeds, then pile the stuffing in the cavity. Red, yellow or orange peppers, top removed and seeds scooped out, work very well too.

(serves 12)

8 round zucchini

2 tbsps olive oil

4 cloves garlic, finely chopped

2 shallots, finely chopped

2 red peppers, finely chopped

8oz/225g goat cheese

1 cup/90g breadcrumbs

½ cup/50g Parmesan or Pecorino

olive oil to drizzle

Cut the tops off each zucchini, scoop out the seedy centers, and discard. Set aside 2 zucchini to chop for the filling.

Heat the olive oil in a frying pan and fry the reserved chopped zucchini, garlic, shallots, and peppers till soft. Tip into a large bowl and mix with goat cheese and breadcrumbs. Stuff each zucchini with the mixture and top with the Parmesan or Pecorino. Drizzle the zucchini with extra olive oil and bake at 425°F/220°C for about 20 minutes or until golden. Cut in half to serve.

joel's artichoke and parmesan dip

Joel makes this dip every time I ask him to and I am always astonished at how something so simple can be so savory. Artichokes from a can or jar are absolutely fine, but once my Italian greengrocer in London had a special on tiny fresh artichokes, so I brought them home and trimmed and marinated them myself. I won't tell you how fantastic they were, because I might never get to do them again.

(serves 6)

8oz/190g artichoke hearts, drained of oil and chopped

1 cup/250ml mayonnaise

1 cup/100g grated Pecorino or Parmesan

Butter a large ramekin or several small ramekins. Mix all ingredients together and spread into the ramekins. Bake at 350°F/180°C for 30 minutes. Serve with crackers or baguette slices.

roasted and smoked salmon herbed mousse

I first ate this a version of this mousse at an elaborate Christmas Fair in London, where it was presented in layers – of mousse and of smoked salmon – and then cut into elegant slices. I have served it this way, and also in dollops on endive or radicchio leaves. The easiest presentation is simply spooned onto toasted baguette slices. It is a very moreish dish, as the British say, meaning that you always want more.

(serves 12)

1½lb/600g fresh salmon fillet

2 tsps olive oil

pinch sea salt and fresh black pepper

7oz/200g cream cheese

7 tbsps/10½oz/300g crème fraîche

handful chives

handful fresh tarragon leaves

handful fresh cilantro/coriander leaves

zest and juice of 1 lemon

sea salt and fresh black pepper to taste

10½oz/300g smoked salmon

3½oz/100g extra crème fraîche

Place the salmon in a foil-lined ovenproof dish and drizzle with olive oil. Season and roast at 425°F/220°C for 25 minutes.

In a food processor, combine the roasted salmon, the cream cheese, crème fraîche, herbs, lemon zest and juice and seasonings. Pulse until well combined but not a mush. Add half the smoked salmon and pulse again. Taste for seasonings and add salt if needed.

For a simple presentation, spread a bit of the mousse on a toasted baguette slice, top with a twist of smoked salmon and a bit of crème fraîche.

everything on crostini

Sometimes when I just don't want to cook a real dinner, we make a meal of these little treats. They are perfect, though, for crowds, as there is something for everyone.

(serves 12)

24 slices baguette

1/3 cup olive oil, more if needed

suggested toppings:

oil-cured Moroccan olives, halved

anchovies melted in butter

pesto

avocado slices

mozzarella

goat cheese

cherry tomatoes

Toast the baguette slices slightly and cool.

Top with any combination of the ingredients above, using the anchovies in butter as a spread, and layering other toppings. Serve warm.

chicken *gribenes*, schmaltz and *rillettes*

These three wonderful uses for chicken thighs represent my fusion of Jewish and French cuisine. I love these dishes because absolutely every part of the thigh – a cut so often unappreciated – is enjoyed.

(serves 12)

6 bone-in, skin-on chicken thighs

2 tbsps duck or goose fat (or rendered schmaltz, even olive oil in a pinch)

1½ cups/375ml chicken stock

3 tbsps Marsala or Madeira wine

1 stem rosemary, leaves only

4 cloves garlic, finely chopped

sea salt and fresh black pepper to taste

To make the *gribenes*, remove skin and fat from thighs. Place in a frying pan in a single layer, or overlapping as little as possible, and cover with ½ cup/125ml water. Place over very low heat and cook at a tiny simmer until the skin is crisp. This will take at least 90 minutes. Remove skin to paper towel and pour the rendered fat, "schmaltz" into a jar to use in this recipe, or to save for another recipe in the fridge.

In a deep saucepan or wok that can accommodate the chicken thighs in a single layer, melt the fat, stock and wine together. Add the rosemary and garlic and season to taste. Place the chicken thighs in the liquid and cook at a simmer, covered, for at least 2 hours. The meat will fall off the bones.

Remove the chicken thighs to a cutting board and allow them to cool so you can handle them. Reserve the cooking liquid. Remove the bones, cartilege and any sinewy bits until you are left with pure chicken. With two forks, shred the meat to a consistency you like, then place in a large bowl. Strain the cooking liquid into a cup (discarding the solids left behind) and pour as much of it over the shredded meat as you need to make the chicken mixture juicy. These are the *rillettes*.

Serve the *rillettes* on crackers, toast, or wrapped in tiny lettuce leaves, topped with the *gribenes*.

chicken liver pâté à la Gladys Taber

This recipe was inspired by the writings of the late, wonderful food and lifestyle writer Gladys Taber, who lived and worked at "Stillmeadow," the white farmhouse across the road from the house we now know as Red Gate Farm, for many years before and after WWII. She understood the beauty of a simple ingredient like chicken livers, which far too many people ignore. I wish I had known Gladys, but I know her descendants who still happily inhabit "Stillmeadow" and visit our dinner table often.

(serves 12)

3 tbsps butter melted

1 small white onion, diced

3 cloves garlic, finely chopped

1 bay leaf

1 pound chicken livers, trimmed of all sinew and membrane

3 tbsps cold butter, cut in 6 pieces

1 tbsp double/heavy cream

2 tbsps brandy or Cognac

sea salt and pepper to taste

Melt the butter in a frying pan wide enough to accommodate the chicken livers in one layer. Cook onion and garlic with bay leaf till vegetables are soft, then remove bay leaf. Add trimmed chicken livers (it isn't important to keep the livers intact when you trim them). Cook just till tender.

Place all in food processor. Turn it on and through the top add, one at a time, the pieces of cold butter, pulsing for a few seconds between each addition, and then the cream and the brandy or cognac. Blend till smooth, then season to taste. Pass through a fine sieve, pressing with a spatula. Discard what remains and pour pâté into three ramekins, 3x1 inch/7x3 cm approximately.

Chill at least 2 hours. Serve with crackers or toasted baguette.

lobster rolls

Whenever our family enjoys steamed Maine lobsters for a summer supper, we buy an extra lobster to make rolls. Some dainty guest usually has a leftover tail as well. Be sure to use rolls without high-fructose corn syrup (not so easy to find as one might hope), because we have learned the hard way that sugar and lobster do not go together.

(serves 4)

2 steamed lobster tails
½ cup/50g celery, finely chopped
½ cup/50g white onion, finely chopped
4 tbsps mayonnaise
chili sauce and lemon juice to taste
sea salt and fresh black pepper to taste
top-split hot dog rolls
chopped chives

Wash the tails thoroughly to remove any green intestine contents and dry with paper towel. Chop the meat into bite-size pieces and mix with the celery, onion, mayonnaise, chili sauce, and lemon juice. Mix thoroughly and season to your taste. Pile generously into the rolls and sprinkle with chives.

eggs benedict with fresh hollandaise

In my experience, no one ever gets enough hollandaise sauce. Perhaps this shortage dates back to the time when people suffered over double boilers with their sauce. My version is simply prepared in a food processor in very little time, and there is no reason not to make plenty.

(serves 12)

6 English muffins, split

12 eggs

12 slices ham

2 batches Hollandaise sauce
  (see recipe p. 223)

chives, finely chopped, to sprinkle

sea salt and fresh black pepper to taste

Toast the English muffins just before serving.

Poach the eggs and suspend in a bath of cold water. Dip in boiling water for a few seconds before serving. This method makes it possible to serve a dozen people at a time.

Sauté the ham until warm.

For each serving, place a slice of ham atop a half English muffin. Top with a warmed poached egg and a generous drizzle of Hollandaise sauce. Sprinkle with chives and season. Serve immediately.

egg pots with ham and Gruyère sauce

This dish is inspired by one of our recent train journeys to visit universities for our daughter. British rail stations, in modern times, have amazingly good food for "takeaways," and one of the best at Kings Cross Station (home of Platform 9¾) is Leon, offering very fresh and healthy food in an instant. On the morning that we went to Edinburgh University, we shared one of these little egg pots, and I immediately made them at home. Perfectly savory.

(serves 12)

12oz/335g cooked ham, shredded
  or chopped roughly
4 tbsps butter
2 tbsps flour
1 pint/500ml whole milk
1½ cups/150g grated Gruyère
pinch cayenne pepper
sea salt and fresh black pepper to taste

Poach or soft-boil the eggs and set aside.

Shred the ham and set aside.

Melt the butter in a heavy saucepan and add the flour, cooking together for a bubbling minute or so. Whisk in the whole milk, whisking constantly and scraping the bottom to get all the floury butter incorporated. Cook this white sauce until thickened. If you feel it is too thick, add a bit of skim milk, whisking all the while.

Add the Gruyère and season with the cayenne, salt and pepper.

Assemble by dipping the eggs in just-boiled water (then crack the top off and scoop out the egg if using soft-boiled). Place either in a large dish, or in individual dishes. Top with ham and pour over sauce. Serve straightaway.

jill's awesome blueberry muffins

My sister brings these to our summer brunches at Red Gate Farm. They are sometimes still warm, and the blueberries often hand-picked by my nieces. They are old-fashioned, simple muffins.

(serves 16)

3 cups/378g plain flour

1 tbsp baking powder

½ tsp baking soda

pinch salt

1 cup/200g white sugar

4oz/113g butter

zest of 2 lemons

2 tbsps vegetable oil

2 eggs

1 cup/250ml sour cream or crème fraîche

½ cup/125ml milk

1 tsp lemon extract

½ tsp vanilla extract

Mix the first four ingredients with a fork. In a large bowl, with an electric mixer, cream the butter and sugar together until fluffy, then add the zest and oil and beat until mixed. Add the eggs one at a time, beating between each. Stir in the sour cream. milk and extracts until well-mixed.

Pour half the dry mixture into the wet and fold just until mixed. Add the second half of the dry mixture and stir gently until just mixed. Fold in the blueberries and spoon into muffin tins lined with muffin paper.

Bake at 375°F/190°C for about 30 minutes, until browned.

avery's Russian blini

Our daughter is happiest in the kitchen wielding a camera, not a whisk, but she came home from a summer adventure in the Russian countryside with this recipe, and enough confidence to try them at home for guests. These may be served plain with butter, or savoury, with sour cream, smoked salmon and beetroot, or sweet, with honey or jam. They are traditionally folded in fourths, but they roll nicely too. Our beautiful neighbor Abigail managed to eat six.

(makes enough for 6 people)

1½ cups/190g plain flour

1 cup/125g buckwheat flour

4 eggs

large pinch salt

small pinch sugar

3 cups/720ml milk

1 tbsp vegetable oil

butter for the pan

Simply whisk everything together thoroughly, then melt butter in a very large frying pan and ladle in enough batter to coat the bottom of the pan, no more.

Cook until easily loosened from pan with a rubber spatula or wooden spoon, then flip or turn over, as your braveness indicates.

thanksgiving stuffing with fresh sage, sausage and cream

This recipe is one of our family's favorites for both Thanksgiving and Christmas dinner. The dish was inspired by the great food writer Laurie Colwin, who said in her marvelous *Home Cooking* that while she herself had never before liked stuffing, a recipe calling for "butter, cream, sweet Italian sausage, mushrooms, celery, garlic, fresh sage and the torn-out insides of two loaves of Italian bread," could not be bad.

(serves 12)

2 large loaves of Italian white bread, torn into bite-size pieces (this amount of bread will weigh in total about 3½lb/1½kg, or enough to fill a casserole dish of 11x13x3inches/ 27x33x7cm)

4oz/112g butter

4 cloves garlic, finely chopped

1 white onion, finely chopped

4 stalks celery, chopped

8 medium mushrooms, chopped

12 leaves fresh sage, chopped

1lb/400g pork sausagemeat

1 cup/240ml cream

2 cup/480ml chicken stock, more if needed

2 eggs, whisked

If you possibly can, two nights before you want to eat it, tear the insides of the bread into little bite-size pieces. Leave to get stale, tossing now and then. It is absolutely essential to do this at least the day before, so that the bread can dry enough to absorb the liquid when the dressing is assembled.

The day before Thanksgiving, if you can (the flavors are so much better if they can rest together overnight), make the dressing. Sauté the garlic, onion, celery, mushrooms and sage in the butter.

Meanwhile, sauté the sausage. When fully cooked, put it through the food processor briefly to break it into uniform pieces. Pour the vegetable mixture and the sausage onto the bread, add the cream and at least two cups of stock plus the eggs, and begin mixing. Add more stock as you need it. The mixture should be wet, but not seeping liquid.

Pat into a buttered 11x13x3inch/23x33x3cm pan, and leave overnight in the fridge. Pat extra butter over the surface and bake just before serving, 45 minutes at 375°F/190°C.

sauces & dressings

Take a quick look in the door of your refrigerator. If you're like me, you store a lot of condiments there, sauces and dressings and spreads of various kinds. Believe me when I say that they are full of preservatives, stabilizers and the like, definitely breaking my ironclad rule of never eating anything I can't pronounce. I was upset when I discovered this, and I obsessed for some time until I had a recipe for each of the condiments I really cared about. Perhaps you won't want to make all your own sauces and dressings, but with this chapter, you can.

The only condiment I never made again, after my experiment, was mustard as it just was not worth the effort and most prepared mustards are only minimally preserved. Measurements have been rounded up for convenience, and unless indicated otherwise, each recipe makes about 1 cup/240ml.

teriyaki sauce

½ cup/120ml soy sauce

¼ cup/60ml mirin

¼ cup/60ml honey

3 tbsps/40ml sesame oil

zest and juice of 1 lime

2-inch piece ginger, peeled and grated

2 cloves garlic, very finely chopped

Mix all in a saucepan and simmer till the sauce bubbles like a toffee, perhaps 5 minutes.

plum sauce

1 cup/325g plum jam or plum preserves

2 tbsps rice wine vinegar

1 tbsp onion, finely chopped

2 tsps honey

1 tsp fresh ginger, grated

1 garlic clove, finely chopped

½ teaspoon crushed red pepper flakes

pinch of salt

Mix all ingredients and simmer in a small saucepan for about five minutes, whisking constantly. If the sauce is not used right away, it may stiffen, and can be resurrected with a little very hot or boiling water.

hollandaise sauce

2 large egg yolks or 3 medium egg yolks
1 cup/226g butter, melted and hot
2 tbsps lemon juice
sea salt to taste

Put the egg yolks in the blender of food
processor and blend at low speed just to mix.
Then, keeping the blender going, add the
boiling water and then the butter, slowly. Add
the lemon juice and salt, keeping the machine
going all the time. If the sauce feels too thick,
just add a trickle of boiling water and process
again. When making Eggs Benedict, assemble
the muffin, bacon and egg and process the
Hollandaise once more just before serving.

Now, if you want to turn this already perfect
sauce into the more festive mousseline, fold
in gently about ½ cup whipped double cream
RIGHT before serving. Don't add it ahead of
time or the sauce will get runny.

tartare sauce

1 cup/240ml mayonnaise
¼ medium red onion, finely chopped
1 tbsp chopped capers
1 tbsp chopped cornichons
1 tsp fresh, chopped tarragon
1 tsp fresh, chopped chives
juice of 1 lemon or lime
plenty of fresh black pepper

Mix all and chill.

barbecue sauce

(makes about 2 cups)

¼ cup/55g each papaya, pineapple and mango

1-inch piece ginger, grated

4 cloves garlic

2 stems fresh thyme, leaves only

1 small red chili

¼ cup/60ml ketchup

¼ cup/60ml Worcestershire sauce

¼ cup/60ml dark molasses

¼ cup/60ml hot sauce (Sriracha or similar)

several shakes Tabasco

juice and zest of 1 lime

good pinch paprika

Whizz the papaya, pineapple, mango, ginger, garlic, thyme, and chili in a food processor.

Whisk all the remaining ingredients together and pour into a saucepan with the mixture in the food processor. Simmer for about 15 minutes until thick.

spicy mayonnaise

1 egg yolk

¼ tsp salt

pinch cayenne

pinch white pepper

pinch dry mustard

juice of half lemon

1 cup/240ml olive oil

1 tbsp Tabasco sauce, or other chili sauce, to taste

With a wire whisk, beat egg yolk with salt, cayenne, pepper and mustard until thick and yellow as a lemon. Then add half the lemon juice slowly and beat again.

Now, one drop at a time for about a minute, add olive oil. Then after the first minute, a steady but TINY stream of oil will do, whisking constantly until the oil is used up. Now whisk in remaining lemon juice slowly.

Chill, and enjoy.

anchovy mint dressing

(makes about ½ cup)

½ cup/60ml olive oil

juice of 1 lemon

1 clove garlic

6 fillets anchovy, rinsed if preserved in salt

10 mint leaves

fresh black pepper

1 tsp fresh mayonnaise

I know this combination sounds a bit daft, but it works like crazy.

Simply place all ingredients in a small blender or mortar and blend until smooth.

poppy seed dressing

½ cup/120ml olive oil

¼ cup/60ml apple cider vinegar

juice and zest of 1 lemon

1 tbsp unrefined sugar

2 tbsps sour cream

1 tbsp mayonnaise

2 tbsps poppy seeds

sea salt to taste

fresh black pepper

Whisk all ingredients for dressing together and toss with the cabbage, carrots and fennel. Serve ice-cold.

blue cheese dressing

½ cup/120ml sour cream
½ cup/120ml mayonnaise
½ tsp Worcestershire sauce
dash garlic powder
dash salt
dash black pepper
3oz/84g blue cheese, crumbled

Mix all ingredients well with a whisk, then fold in crumbled blue cheese. Chill.

satay sauce

(makes about 2 cups)

1 x 14oz/400ml can coconut milk
½ cup/125g crunchy peanut butter
½ small onion, grated
1 tbsp dark soy sauce
2 teaspoons brown sugar
½ teaspoon red pepper flakes
1 tsp ground turmeric

Boil all ingredients at a low boil for three minutes and set aside to cool.

paris butter

8oz/225g butter
1 tbsp each: garlic, shallots, cornichons, capers, fresh tarragon, fresh thyme, fresh dill, fresh chives, fresh rosemary, tomato paste, pine nuts, brandy, madeira
1 tsp each: Dijon mustard, lemon zest, anchovy
dash fish sauce, Worcester sauce, Tabasco
1 pinch each: curry powder, cayenne pepper, paprika, celery salt, ground cumin
juice of ½ lemon
sea salt and pepper

Simply throw everything into a food processor or blender and mix until completely smooth. Roll in foil in a cylinder shape and freeze.

Once thawed, a coin-sized piece of this butter melts perfectly on a grilled steak, chicken breast fillet or salmon fillet. Melted, it is lovely on popcorn.

desserts

Those who know me well know that I do not have a sweet tooth. I also find it difficult to follow strict instructions, and so baking is a real challenge for me. For all these reasons, my dessert repertoire is limited, and almost exclusively to recipes that talented friends have baked for me and shared.

While not wanting very often to cook sweet things for myself, I always enjoy the desserts made for me by these generous friends. Therefore, when dinner guests ask, "What can I bring?" I never say, "Oh, just bring yourself." I specify the sweet thing that I associate with that person, and then sit back in total relaxation, knowing that I am off the hook for dessert and that we are in for a treat.

fely's banana and apple spiced cake

Fely was the trusted babysitter and housekeeper of one of Avery's childhood friends, whose mother hosted a writing group in her sunny London sitting room once a month. At one of our meetings, Fely brought in a tray carrying coffee and this cake, warm from the oven. The aroma – at once intensely spicy and fruity – was spectacular. After our group broke up that afternoon, I pursued Fely into the kitchen and asked for the recipe. I have made this cake many, many times with perfect results, and I have brought wedges of it with me when visiting sick people, people with small children and people in need of a boost. It is foolproof (I am the fool in question) and absolutely delicious.

(serves 8)

1½ cups/180g plain flour

1 tsp baking soda

1 tsp baking powder

½ tsp each ground cinnamon, cloves and nutmeg

pinch sea salt

½ cup/113g butter, softened

1 cup/200g sugar

2 eggs

½ tsp vanilla

about 1 cup/120g/2 medium mashed bananas

about 1 cup/120g/2 medium chopped apples

1 tbsp confectioner's sugar

Combine all dry ingredients except the confectioner's sugar. In another bowl, cream butter and sugar, eggs and vanilla. Mix together dry and wet ingredients and add mashed banana and chopped apple. Bake at 350°F/180°C for 45 minutes. Cool slightly and dust with sugar. Serve warm.

elizabeth's lemon polenta cake
(with or without blueberries)

This is my official birthday cake. I love it for its crunch and intense lemony flavour, and because my friend Elizabeth bakes it for me whenever I ask. It's lovely to have a gluten-free dessert idea on hand. I will never forget one dinner party where the cake sat, during the main course, at the end of our long dining table. When dessert time came, I found my small tabby cat with her face in the cake, having eaten a good 2-inch circle as we had our dinner. I ate the "catty" piece, being a good hostess. It just goes to show that absolutely anyone will love this cake. I like to add blueberries for my mother's birthday party.

(serves 8)

1 cup/225g butter, softened

1 cup/225g sugar

2¼ cups/225g ground almonds

2 tsps vanilla extract

3 eggs

zest of 4 lemons

juice of 1 lemon

1 cup/125g cornmeal/polenta

1½ tsps baking powder

pinch sea salt

1 cup/100g blueberries, if using

Butter and flour a 12-inch/30cm springform or plain round cake pan. It does not need to be particularly deep.

Beat the butter and sugar together until pale and light. Stir in the ground almonds and vanilla. Beat in the eggs, one at a time. Fold in the lemon zest and lemon juice, the polenta, baking powder and salt.

Scrape the batter into the pan and scatter the blueberries, if using, on top. Bake at 350°F/180°C for 45–55 minutes. Test with a toothpick or skewer in the center; if it comes out clean, the cake is done. The center may seem jiggly, but the sides of the cake should have come away a bit from the tin. Check frequently to make sure the top does not burn; it should have a deep golden brown color, but not blackened.

judy's lavender cookies

My friend Judy lives up the road from Red Gate Farm and keeps a careful eye on the house when we are away, and on us when we are there. Last summer Avery contracted Lyme disease, a hazard of life in the Connecticut countryside and spent an awful two weeks with its symptoms alone in Washington, D.C., at a political conference. When she got home to us and was diagnosed, she took to bed with her headache and fever. Judy came by with these cookies and a sympathetic hug. They are classic sugar cookies with a floral twist, a bit like Judy herself.

(makes about 3 dozen)

½ cup/113g butter

1 cup/225g sugar

2 eggs

½ tsp vanilla extract

2 tsp lavender blossoms

1½ cup/180g flour

2 tsp baking powder

Cream butter and sugar together until fluffy. Beat in eggs and vanilla and lavender blossoms. In a separate bowl, mix flour and baking powder. Stir into lavender mixture. Drop by teaspoons onto baking sheet and bake at 350°F/180°C 8–10 minutes, until edges are browned. Cool completely.

nonna's cappuccino cookies

My mother-in-law Rosemary is one of the best cooks I know, and thankfully also one of the best bakers. She comes to visit us in London and at Red Gate Farm armed with a towering stack of cookie tins filled with her specialities, with charming Iowa names like "snickerdoodles," and "lime meltaways." But the most popular of her cookies are these: buttery, crisp and intense, flavoured with coffee, yet beloved by small children. Once she brought them to us in a tall narrow tin that had once held a bottle of John's dad's very fine Scotch.

(makes about 4 dozen)

1 cup/225g butter, softened

½ cup plus 2 tbsps/112g sugar

1 egg yolk

1 tbsp freeze-dried instant coffee

1 tbsp cocoa powder

1 tsp ground cinnamon

¾ tsp salt

1 cup/120g cake flour

1 cup/120g white flour

½ cup/64g mini chocolate chips
   or chocolate put through food
   processor to small bits

Cream butter till fluffy. Add sugar and cream again. Mix coffee, cocoa, cinnamon and salt in a small dish. Add by small amounts to butter and sugar mixture and mix well. Mix two flours and add gradually to butter and sugar mixture. Stir in chips with a spatula.

Divide dough into thirds and roll each third onto parchment paper in 1-inch logs. Chill 1 hour. Bake at 350°F/180°C for about 8 minutes.

avery's peanut butter brownie with cream cheese frosting

When Avery gets stressed, as happens to some degree during exam periods, she bakes. Sometimes she gets her friend Maddie to help in this, and their shouts of laughter from the kitchen are a very soothing sound. For this recipe, Avery and I worked together, inspired by a lovely blog called "The Brown-Eyed Baker." We felt instinctively that her quantities would yield a too-sweet result for my taste, and so we greatly reduced the amount of sugar in the bottom two layers. These brownies are very American-tasting, very chocolatey, and last for quite awhile, especially if you store them in the fridge.

(makes 36 very small brownies)

for brownie base:

⅓ cup/40g cocoa powder

1 tbsp freeze-dried instant coffee

½ cup plus 2 tbsps/118ml boiling water

2oz/57g chocolate, finely chopped

4 tbsps butter, melted

½ cup plus 2 tbsps/118ml vegetable oil

2 eggs

2 egg yolks

2 tsps vanilla extract

1½ cups/300g sugar

1¾ cups/220g flour

¾ tsp sea salt

for middle layer:

¾ cup/190g smooth peanut butter

½ cup/113g unsalted butter

pinch sea salt

1 cup/128g powdered (confectioner's)
    sugar

2 tbsps whole milk

1 tsp vanilla extract

for frosting layer:

12oz/340g chocolate

½ cup/113g smooth peanut butter

Line a 9x13inch/23x33cm baking dish with foil, folding the foil up over all the sides and edges. Butter the bottom.

Whisk cocoa, espresso powder and boiling water together in large bowl until smooth. Add unsweetened chocolate and whisk until chocolate is melted. Whisk in melted butter and oil. (Mixture may look curdled.) Add eggs, yolks, and vanilla and continue to whisk until smooth. Whisk in sugar until fully incorporated. Add flour and salt and mix with rubber spatula until just combined.

Scrape batter into prepared pan and bake for 30–35 minutes. Allow to cool 1½ hours.

Meanwhile, beat together the peanut butter, butter and salt with an electric mixer on medium speed until smooth and creamy, about 2 minutes. Reduce the speed to low and alternate adding the powdered sugar and the milk in thirds, mixing to combine after each addition. Add the vanilla extract, beat to combine, then increase the speed to medium-high and beat until completely smooth and creamy. Spread the peanut butter mixture in an even layer over the top of the cooled brownie layer.

Melt together the chocolate chips and peanut butter in a bowl over a pan of simmering water. Pour the mixture over the peanut butter layer and spread into an even layer. Refrigerate for at least 30 minutes, or until set.

Holding on to the foil edges, lift the solid brownies out onto a cutting board and cut into 36 squares, or larger if you like. Store in the refrigerator.

rosie's celestial chocolate amaretto mousse

Years ago, I spent five days in the Devon countryside with a group of aspiring food writers on an Arvon Foundation course. There we agonized, scribbled, underwent criticism from our tutors that spared no feelings, and somehow had a wonderful time. A small group of us, "Gathering Nuts in May," has reunited every year to share a house in the country and devote ourselves to shopping for food, cooking, eating and talking about all of the above. The glue that binds us together is our friend Rosie, the Silver Fox, one of the most generous people I will ever know. This is her famous dessert.

(serves 6)

2oz/60g amaretto biscuits
(approximately 12), crushed

6oz/150g chocolate

1 tbsp salted butter, or unsalted plus
pinch salt

1 tbsp strong espresso coffee

1 tbsp amaretto liqueur

4 eggs, separated

1 tbsp sugar

1¼ cups/300ml heavy/double cream

In a large attractive serving bowl, or in individual dessert dishes, scatter half the biscuit crumbs. Melt the chocolate in a bowl placed over simmering water, then stir in the butter, coffee and amaretto. Set aside to cool.

Whisk the egg whites with an electric mixer or by hand until stiff. Set aside. Whisk the egg yolks and sugar together until pale, thickened, creamy and about doubled in volume, and set aside. Whip the cream until just whipped.

Fold the egg whites into the chocolate mixture, then fold in the yolk mixture, followed by the whipped cream. Pour into desired serving dish or dishes and scatter remaining crumbs on top. Refrigerate for at least 8 hours or overnight. Serve with fresh berries and more whipped cream if liked. A glass of amaretto on the side would be lovely as well.

suzanne's peach trifle

I love this recipe partly because it is summery and delicious, but partly because the way it is written perfectly reflects my friend Suzanne, who has graced my dinner table in London many times with her husband John. Suzanne lives life with exuberance and energy and that is just how this dish sounds on the page. English "trifle" always involves an element of biscuits or cake soaked in alcohol, fruit, and whipped cream. If you have difficulty finding amaretti biscuits, any other simple crunchy cookie you like will do. Equally, Grand Marnier or Cointreau will fill in for the amaretto if that is what you have on hand.

(serves 4)

1½ cup/150g amaretti biscuits

3 tsps amaretto (or sherry)

6 fresh peaches, peeled and sliced
   (or high quality canned peaches)

1 cup/250ml heavy/double cream,
   whipped

handful flaked almonds

Crush biscuits and drizzle with amaretto. Put in a pretty bowl, add peaches and cream. Chill. Scatter almonds. Voila!

mini cheesecakes with chocolate chips and a fresh raspberry glaze

Avery used to spend her summers in Connecticut fostering kittens from a nearby shelter, and then finding homes for them. A year ago we spent an afternoon going through the various stages of making these cheesecakes and photographing them at the picnic table. When we finished shooting the cheesecakes, we put them in the refrigerator and replaced them on the table with kittens, tiny and staggering. It was a dream afternoon, full of sweetness and softness.

(makes about 2 dozen, half chocolate and half fruit)

2 cups/200g graham crackers, or digestive biscuits, crushed fine

½ cup/113g butter, melted

2 packages/500g cream cheese, room temperature

3 eggs, room temperature

¾ cup/95g sugar

1 tsp vanilla extract

zest of 1 lime and 1 lemon

2 cups/450ml light/half-fat sour cream

2 cups/340g mini chocolate chips/chocolate pulsed in a food processor till chip-like

1 cup/100g blackberries

1 cup/100g strawberries

½ cup/118ml water

¼ cup/50g sugar

Mix the cookie crumbs and the melted butter with a fork, fluffing lightly. Line a muffin tin with muffin papers, then place a tablespoon of the cookie mixture in each and press down with your fingers. Place in the fridge and chill while you prepare the other ingredients.

With an electric hand mixer, beat the cream cheese for a minute or so to make sure there aren't lumps. Add the eggs one at a time, beating at a low speed between each and scraping the sides of the bowl. Add the sugar, vanilla and zests and beat for 1 minute more. Add the half-fat sour cream and beat for another minute. Do not let it get frothy.

Fill each muffin cup nearly to the top and sprinkle mini chocolate chips on half. Place in the center of the oven and bake at 350°F/180°C for about 20–25 minutes, until the cheesecakes are stiff but still jiggly. Carefully remove the paper sleeves from the muffin tray and chill in the fridge for at least two hours.

Place the berries, water and sugar in a saucepan and cook over medium heat, mashing with a potato masher. Pass this mixture through a coarse sieve into a bowl. When the cheesecakes are all cooked and cooled, drizzle the plain cheesecakes with the berry coulis.

gerada's oklahoma pecan pie

Several years ago, friends of friends asked to borrow Red Gate Farm for their family Thanksgiving, and since it was sitting empty, we were happy to say yes. Anne, George and their children had often stayed in the farmhouse across the road, and had happy memories of our dusty, white picket fence part of the world. Because they were such gracious guests, we became friends in the virtual way that modern people do, exchanging many emails and messages over the years. Last Thanksgiving, a heavy brown box arrived from Anne's mother, far away in Oklahoma: pecans from their tree, and a perfect recipe for pecan pie. This was a novel dessert for our British guests, and we all ate it happily, thinking of the beauty of friendship, stretching across the pond.

(serves 8)

1¹/₃ cups/160g plain flour

¾ tsp salt

¹/₃ cup/78ml vegetable oil

¼ cup/60ml cold milk

3 eggs

1 cup/236ml light corn syrup
(Karo or Lyle's)

½ cup/100g sugar

1 tbsp plain flour

2 tbsps very soft butter

1 tsp vanilla

dash sea salt

1 cup/110g coarsely chopped pecans

½ cup/55g whole, perfect pecans

In a medium bowl, mix flour and salt. Stir milk and oil together in a cup and then pour onto flour mixture. Mix dough until it leaves the sides of the bowl. Roll out the dough into a circle about 12 inches/30cm wide for a 9-inch/22cm pie. Lay the pie pan over the crust and flip it over. Press into the pan and press the edges with a dinner knife to decorate, or flute the crust.

Lightly beat the eggs, then stir in the remaining ingredients, except the whole pecans. Pour the mixture into the pie crust then decorate with the whole pecans. Cover the crust edges with foil to keep from burning. Bake at 375°F/190°C for about 40 minutes, then remove foil to let edges brown. Baker a further 15 minutes until filling has set and the pie is a deep golden brown.

nora's pumpkin pie

Our friends Nora and Tom began gracing our Thanksgiving celebrations with just their first little boy, and now there are two. The day wouldn't be complete without Otis and Artie now, nor this classic pie which Nora is kind enough to bring every year. Our English friends are always happy to have this most humble of pies, a true American treat.

(serves 8)

1⅓ cup/160g plain flour

¾ tsp salt

⅓ cup/78ml vegetable oil

¼ cup/60ml cold milk

¾ cup granulated sugar

1 teaspoon ground cinnamon

½ teaspoon salt

½ teaspoon ground ginger

¼ teaspoon ground cloves

2 large eggs

1 x 15oz/400g can pure pumpkin purée

1 x 12oz/350ml can evaporated milk

1 cup/240ml whipping cream

½ tsp vanilla extract

Mix flour with salt in a large bowl. Mix oil and milk in a smaller bowl, then pour into flour and mix well until dough comes away from the bowl. Roll out the dough into a circle about 12 inches/30cm wide for a 9-inch/22cm pie. Lay the pie pan over the crust and flip it over. Press into the pan and press the edges with a dinner knife to decorate, or flute the crust.

Mix all remaining ingredients except whipping cream and vanilla extract, and pour into pie dish. Bake at 425°F/220°C for 15 minutes, then reduce temperature to 350°F/180°C and bake for a further 20–30 minutes or until center is set and a toothpick comes out clean.

Whip cream with vanilla and serve the pie warm with the cream on top.

Thanksgiving menu

herb-brined roasted turkey (see recipe p. 80)

honey-roasted ham (see recipe p. 105)

thanksgiving stuffing (see recipe p. 218)

becky's cheesy potatoes (see recipe p. 131)

dashiell hammett spinach (see recipe p. 141)

caramelized carrots (see recipe p. 162)

green beans (see recipe p. 165)

gerada's oklahoma pecan pie (see recipe p. 247)

nora's pumpkin pie (see recipe p. 248)

Thanksgiving

Thanksgiving is a favorite holiday in our family, all the more so since we moved to England. We feel quite homesick on the day, just an ordinary Thursday in our adopted home, with family and friends at school and work, unlike the day-long holiday it is in America. We tend to gather around our table any lonely Americans we can find, and British friends who are intrigued by the notion of a holiday centered entirely on food and thankfulness. While we miss the football and parades that we'd be watching on television if we were 'home,' we love bringing the delicious traditional foods to our London table.

The menu to the left will provide something for everyone on the day, and can easily be used as a Christmas menu as well.

index